# RAM OULA

# Emerge

*21 Daily Devotions and Prayers To Activate Your Best Self In Christ*

# Contents

# Dedication

This devotional is dedicated to my three precious daughters, Elvira, Ziona and Briella. You girls are the lights of my life and the inspiration behind every word I've written. Your presence in my life has been a profound blessing, a gift from God that continually reminds me of His grace and love.

You inspire me each day to draw closer to God, and to strive for excellence. Your existence is a daily call to leave a legacy, to reach for the highest ideals, and to be a reflection of the love and faith that we hold dear.

I am also eternally grateful to my Lord Jesus Christ, who has inspired me to use my gifts, to write, and to be an inspiration to others.  It is through His guidance and grace that I have embarked on this journey, and my prayer is that this devotional will impact lives and set people free.

As I pen these words, my heartfelt prayer is that one day my girls will read this devotional and draw inspiration from it. May they find in its pages not only knowledge but also the fuel to pursue their own purpose in their own time, and grow to become the best versions of themselves in Christ.

May they grow to become examples to others in the unique ways God has called them to be and discover their life's purpose. May God bless and guide them always, and may this book be a small contribution to their journey towards becoming the remarkable individuals I know they are destined to be.

# Preface

Hello to all the curious minds embarking on a journey of self-discovery and growth! Buckle up, because we're about to explore the exciting idea of becoming the best version of you. But guess what? It's not a walk in the park. Nope, not at all. It's more like climbing a mountain – tough, but oh-so-worth-it. Why? Well, because it's one of the most important things you can do for yourself.

Here's the scoop: Life isn't always a smooth ride. It throws curve balls and disappointments our way, leaving us with unmet expectations that can really make us stop and think. It's like a puzzle, where we try to figure out why we're feeling stressed or anxious. The process is about building boundaries—like creating a safe space for yourself, your thoughts, and your overall well-being. Think of it as drawing a line to keep the things that stress you out at bay. Life, my friends, is like a gift we've all been handed. But here's the twist: what we do with that gift is totally up to us. We have the power to live a life that's full of happiness, safety, and the kind of life that lines up with what Christ would want for us.

Speaking of Christ, have you heard the verse, *"Knock and the door shall be opened unto you?"* (Matthew 7:7-12) Well, guess what? That's like a hint from God that boundaries are kind of a big deal. As a child of God, here's a nugget of wisdom: you matter, and you don't need to carry everyone else's troubles on your shoulders. You're unique, you're special, and nobody can tell you otherwise.

Ready for the big finale? I used to react super fast when life threw me a curve ball. But now, I've learned the art of hitting pause. I take a breather and think about how my choices will affect me, my health, and my relationship with God. After this quick reflection, I make decisions with confidence, knowing that fear doesn't define me. Nope, it's all about strength and having a clear mind.

So, as we navigate this adventure called life, remember this: it's okay to focus on you. Tune into that inner voice, lean into your spiritual side, and most importantly, take care of yourself. Get ready to dive deep, uncover hidden treasures within, and embrace the journey of becoming the best you possible! be self full, let your cup flow over so that you can poor into other people cup the way God intended it to be. You are the apple of his eyes and You too matter to him.

Welcome to a journey of self-discovery, transformation, and spiritual growth. Within the pages of this devotional, you will embark on an exploration your capacity to rise above challenges, embrace purpose, and connect with God.

The chapters that follow offer a roadmap for your personal and spiritual development. Each chapter is a stepping stone on your path to becoming the best version of yourself, to emerge from the depths of your experiences with newfound strength and wisdom.

In "Unveiling the Power of Surroundings," we delve into the profound impact of our environment on our well-being and growth. You'll discover how to harness the power of your surroundings to nurture your soul.

"Energizing Your Essence by Channeling Life's Purpose"

guides you in aligning your actions with your life's purpose, energizing your very essence and inviting a sense of fulfillment into your daily life.

In "Minding Your Business is Free," we explore the simplicity and beauty of minding our own business, letting go of unnecessary burdens, and focusing on what truly matters.

"Boundaries Unleashed by Nurturing Divine Balance" teaches you how to establish healthy boundaries that honor your well-being while maintaining a connection with God.

"Soul's Sanctuary by Discovering God's Presence" invites you to seek solace in the presence of God, creating a sanctuary within yourself where you can find peace and strength.

"The Journey Inward: A Dance of Self-Love" is a celebration of self-love and self-discovery. Embrace the beauty of who you are and embark on a transformative inward journey.

"Triumphing Beyond Men: Trusting God's Plan" encourages you to trust in God's plan and rise above societal expectations, finding strength in your unique path.

"Embracing My Unique Journey" emphasizes the importance of embracing your individual journey and recognizing your distinct path to personal and spiritual growth.

"Trusting God's Plan through Pain" explores the power of faith during times of pain and adversity. Learn how faith can guide you through life's most challenging moments.

"Emerging from Emotional Scars to a Healthy Mental Health" is a guide to healing emotional scars and nurturing your mental well-being, emerging stronger and healthier.

"Boundaries Are Your Friends" inspires you to embrace your authenticity and empowers you to live your truth, unapologetically.

"Loving Yourself Requires Hard Work" delves into the essential work of self-love, reminding you that self-love is a journey that requires dedication and commitment.

"Embracing a Future Beyond Present Worries" offers guidance on releasing worries about the future, allowing you to step confidently into the unknown.

"Birthing Alignment with Wisdom, Strategy, and Prayer" explores the power of alignment with divine wisdom and strategy, facilitated by prayer.

"Stepping into a Season of Glory and New Dimensions" invites you to step into a new season of life, filled with glory and the promise of new dimensions of spiritual growth.

"Embracing The Wilderness: Perseverance in Spiritual Dryness" provides insights into navigating periods of spiritual dryness, emerging with renewed vitality.

"My Tiny Seed" emphasizes the importance of prayer as a means of connecting with God's wisdom.

"The Power of Prayer And Discernment" explores the transformative power of prayer and the discernment that comes with a deep spiritual connection.

"The Divine Invitation: Birthing Your Purpose" encourages you to answer Jesus's call to birth your unique purpose into the world.

"Pain in Purpose" discusses the valuable lessons found in pain and hardship, demonstrating how they can be integral to your purpose.

"Legacy of Faith: Passing the Torch of Belief" closes our journey by encouraging you to build a legacy of faith and pass on the torch of belief to future generations.

As you delve into these chapters, may you find inspiration, guidance, and the tools to navigate your own unique journey of self-discovery and spiritual growth. Embrace the lessons within, and may you emerge from this book with renewed purpose and a deeper connection with our Lord Jesus.

# 1

# Unveiling The Power Of Surroundings

In the journey of life, there comes a moment where we must hit the pause button, taking a moment to delve deep within ourselves and truly embrace our place in this vast universe. It is crucial to connect with the very essence of the space we occupy, devoting a moment of introspection to recognize the profound significance of the "who," "what," and "where" that shape our existence. We must be mindful of those around us—people who share our environment, impact us, and hold significant influence.

This contemplation bears tremendous significance as we assess the individuals we allow into our space. We must discern the ones who enter without our permission, those who have been invited, and, crucially, those whose presence affects not just ourselves but our bond with God. Our most vital relationship with our Lord Jesus rests upon our ability to discern and understand the surrounding environment—the factors that may hinder or nurture that connection. Unsafe people may infiltrate our lives, even among friends and family, requiring careful discernment on who we allow into our realm and for how long. Some may prove trustworthy in business matters, yet detrimental to our mental well-being. Hence, it falls upon our shoulders to take charge, set healthy boundaries, and recognize our God-given worth despite any others who may suggest otherwise.

Every person we encounter possesses a distinct role in shaping our emotions and ultimately influencing our relationship with Jesus. To deepen that connection, we must extend our awareness beyond the individuals themselves and consider the larger community we have willingly embraced. As we engage in self-reflection, we may realize that we have ventured into new realms, inviting further exploration of our surroundings and the implications they hold. In doing so, we continue to unveil the profound truth that we are fearfully and wonderfully made, questioning any voices within our circle that may contradict this biblical reality.

Maintaining healthy boundaries in relationships and within your environment is crucial for safeguarding your spiritual well-being. Your journey with our Lord Jesus is of paramount importance, guiding your day-to-day life and infusing it with profound meaning. To protect this sacred journey, several key principles come into play:

- Begin with self-awareness, delving deep into your own values, beliefs, and spiritual goals. Just as a financial advisor assesses your financial values to guide your investments, understanding your values and beliefs serves as a compass for your spiritual investments.

- Clear communication is essential; articulate your values with love and clarity. Ensure that those around you comprehend what you hold dear and why you prioritize your spiritual journey.

- Recognize the power of saying "no" as an act of self-care and protection, rather than a negative response. Safeguarding your relationship with Christ may require this decisive step at times.

- Respect the significance of your time. Let your "yes" align with your spiritual priorities, and allow your "no" to shield your spiritual well-being.

- Seek support and guidance from mentors, counselors, or individuals who grasp the depth of your commitment to your spiritual journey. Surrounding yourself with like-minded individuals provides invaluable support.

- Understand that seasons and commitments in life have expiration dates, just as relationships and situations evolve. Embrace the flexibility of your boundaries and priorities as they naturally shift over time.

In essence, it is essential to wholeheartedly acknowledge, comprehend, and remain aware of the people we have intertwined our lives with. Each person can shape our emotions and significantly impact our relationship with Jesus. As we navigate this intricate journey, let us remember to tread consciously within the circles we have joined, ever seeking alignment with our true selves and the divine presence of our Lord Jesus.

**Scriptures:**

Matthew 22:37-39:

*"Jesus said to him, 'You shall love the Lord your God with all your heart, with all your soul, and with all your mind.' This is the first and great commandment. And the second is like it: 'You shall love your neighbor as yourself.'"*

Proverbs 12:26:

*"The righteous should choose his friends carefully, for the way of the wicked leads them astray."*

Proverbs 13:20:

*"He who walks with wise men will be wise, but the companion of fools will be destroyed."*

2 Corinthians 6:14:

*"Do not be yoked together with unbelievers. For what do righteousness and wickedness have in common? Or what fellowship can light have with darkness?"*

Proverbs 18:24:

*"One who has unreliable friends soon comes to ruin, but there is a friend who sticks closer than a brother."*

Psalm 1:1-3:

*"Blessed is the man who walks not in the counsel of the ungodly, nor stands in the path of sinners, nor sits in the seat of the scornful; but his delight is in the law of the Lord, and in His law he meditates day and night. He shall be*

*like a tree planted by the rivers of water, that brings forth its fruit in its season, whose leaf also shall not wither; and whatever he does shall prosper."*

1 Corinthians 15:33:

*"Do not be deceived: 'Evil company corrupts good habits.'"*

Proverbs 27:9:

*"Ointment and perfume delight the heart, and the sweetness of a man's friend gives delight by hearty counsel."*

Ecclesiastes 4:9-10:

*"Two are better than one, because they have a good reward for their labor. For if they fall, one will lift up his companion. But woe to him who is alone when he falls, for he has no one to help him up."*

Proverbs 22:24-25:

*"Make no friendship with an angry man, and with a furious man do not go, lest you learn his ways and set a snare for your soul."*

These scriptures remind us of the importance of choosing our friends and relationships wisely, prioritizing our connection with God, and being aware of the influence others can have on our lives.

**Prayer Points:**

1. Heavenly Father, in the midst of the chaos and busyness of life, I humbly ask for the wisdom and discernment to pause and reflect on my inner self. Grant me the ability to find peace and focus on the space I occupy in this world.

2. Lord, I pray that You open my eyes to recognize the significance of the people surrounding me. Help me discern those who positively impact my life and deepen my relationship with You, while guarding against those who may hinder my spiritual growth. Give me the wisdom to choose my companions wisely.

3. Dear God, reveal to me any unsafe relationships or individuals in my life. Grant me the courage to set healthy boundaries and make wise decisions about who I allow into my sacred space. Guide me to surround myself with people who bring positivity, support, and encouragement.

4. Lord Jesus, I humbly ask for the strength to nurture my bond with You above all else. Help me understand how my relationships and surroundings can either strengthen or hinder my connection with Your divine presence. Grant me the wisdom to prioritize You in every aspect of my life.

5. Heavenly Father, grant me the ability to discern the different roles that people play in my life. Guide me to recognize those who bring positivity, support, and encouragement, and empower me to surround myself with individuals who lift me up and draw me closer to You.

6. Lord, please grant me self-knowledge and awareness to assess my own presence within various circles and communities. Help me understand the influence I have on others and guide me to seek alignment with Your truth in every interaction and relationship.

7. Dear God, I surrender to Your divine guidance in choosing

the people I allow into my life. Teach me to embrace the truth that I am fearfully and wonderfully made, detaching myself from any voices undermining my worth in Your eyes.

8. Heavenly Father, I pray for Your grace to navigate relationships wisely, considering not only their immediate impact but also their lasting effects on my emotional and spiritual well-being. Help me make wise choices that honor You.

9. Lord Jesus, help me cultivate a deep connection with You that goes beyond human relationships. Enable me to prioritize my relationship with You above all else and seek Your presence in every area of my life.

10. Heavenly Father, I entrust my relationships to Your loving hands, seeking Your guidance and protection. Lead me to surround myself with individuals who wholeheartedly support my journey toward spiritual growth and a closer walk with You. May Your divine wisdom be my compass. In Jesus Name, Amen.

Reflect

# 2

# Energizing Your Essence by Channeling Life's Purpose

God's blessings grant us a gift of seven days each week, each day divided into twenty-four precious hours. Among these hours, which one captures your attention the most? How do you spend your time? Is it consumed by sleep or filled with troubling conversations? Do you invest in your own growth and betterment? Do you take moments to connect with Jesus? And who shares in your positive energy? In the grand design of life, our paths cross with others, a fundamental part of being human. Yet, consider this: There are both supportive and harmful people out there.

Do your days revolve around connections with those who spread hatred, negativity, and self-righteousness? These people drain your energy, leaving emptiness behind. Their presence feels heavy and unsteady. Are you entangled with these draining individuals, giving away your vital energy to them? Or do you surround yourself with those who radiate love, kindness, and humility? They listen attentively and value the connections we share.

Indeed, it's important to assess who you allow into your life, as they influence your energy's direction. Places, too, hold power. While you might not always choose your surroundings, wisdom lies in discerning their impact. This awareness can protect you from unnecessary depletion. Where and with whom do you invest your energy and spirit?

Every expenditure of energy should bring returns. Spending time with certain people or in specific places should bring positive outcomes. Reflect: What do you gain from these interactions? Do they nurture you or drain your energy? I'm not suggesting complete isolation but rather finding the balance. Be intentional with your time because intention is key. Every part of your day matters. Every drop of your energy is a choice.

Remember: the Bible teaches us to *"love your neighbor as yourself."* Prioritize yourself. You control your energy's distribution. You decide when to engage, where to direct your efforts, and who deserves your attention. This control is both a privilege and a responsibility.

It's easy to get caught up in the fast-paced demands of life, but I want to urge you to take a step back and dedicate some time for self-reflection. When was the last time you took yourself out on a date, not for the purpose of entertainment, but to ponder the deeper aspects of your existence? Self-reflection offers a precious opportunity to contemplate the meaning and purpose of your life, to assess the activities and relationships that fill your days, and to listen to the whispers of our Lord Jesus in the midst of the chaos.

In these moments of stillness, you can gain valuable insights into what drains your energy, causes stress, or brings negativity into your life. By identifying these sources, you can gradually work towards transforming them into sources of vitality and positivity. Equally important, self-reflection helps you recognize the positive elements that support your boundaries, self-care, and your relationship with Christ.

Think of your energy as a vessel, similar to a car's fuel tank. You wouldn't wait for your tank to be empty before refueling, right? Similarly, you should replenish your energy regularly, seeking activities that bring joy rather than stress. Just as night brings sleep and Ecclesiastes 3:8 reminds us of various times and seasons, including a time for rest, you need to recharge. In order to give, you must first be full. Fill your reservoir through prayer, self-care, and enjoyable activities.

Maybe reading these words is already a moment of recharging for you. Such actions contribute to replenishing your energy. You must do this because you can't share love if you lack it within yourself. You can't offer peace if you don't possess it. Remember the support of the Holy Spirit, which aids you on this journey of renewal.

Remember to draw strength from scripture and continue nurturing your spiritual growth. It's a journey that takes time, but there is hope in the process of transformation. Embrace your own power to bring about renewal and spiritual growth in your life. With dedication and faith, you can navigate this path toward a deeper and more meaningful connection with yourself and with God. Ephesians 5:15-16 advises, *"Look carefully then how you walk, not as unwise but as wise, making the best use of the time, because the days are evil."* In a world filled with challenges and uncertainties, wisdom lies in how you allocate your energy and time. Reflect on the course of your energy, on the people and places you invest in. Go deep, reset, because through these actions, transformation can occur. Let personal growth ignite, let your energy flow with purpose, and may blessings shower upon you.

**Scriptures:**

Psalm 139:23-24:

*"Search me, O God, and know my heart; try me, and know my anxieties; and see if there is any wicked way in me, and lead me in the way everlasting."*

Proverbs 13:20:

*"He who walks with wise men will be wise, but the companion of fools will be destroyed."*

1 Corinthians 15:33:

*"Do not be deceived: 'Evil company corrupts good habits.'"*

Proverbs 4:23:

*"Keep your heart with all diligence, for out of it spring the issues of life."*

1 Corinthians 6:19-20:

*"Or do you not know that your body is the temple of the Holy Spirit who is in you, whom you have from God, and you are not your own? For you were bought at a price; therefore glorify God in your body and in your spirit, which are God's."*

Luke 11:34-36:

*"The lamp of the body is the eye. Therefore, when your*

*eye is good, your whole body also is full of light. But when your eye is bad, your body also is full of darkness. Therefore take heed that the light which is in you is not darkness. If then your whole body is full of light, having no part dark, the whole body will be full of light, as when the bright shining of a lamp gives you light."*

Matthew 11:28-30:

*"Come to Me, all you who labor and are heavy laden, and I will give you rest. Take My yoke upon you and learn from Me, for I am gentle and lowly in heart, and you will find rest for your souls. For My yoke is easy and My burden is light."*

Ecclesiastes 3:1-8:

*"To everything there is a season, a time for every purpose under heaven..."*

Colossians 4:5-6:

*"Walk in wisdom toward those who are outside, redeeming the time. Let your speech always be with grace, seasoned with salt, that you may know how you ought to answer each one."*

Philippians 4:13:

*"I can do all things through Christ who strengthens me."*

**Prayer Points:**

1. Heavenly Father, I am grateful for the gift of seven days each week and the precious hours within them. Thank you for the opportunity to experience life and time's rhythm.

2. Lord, grant me wisdom to discern where to invest my time and energy. Help me make intentional choices that align with your purpose for my life.

3. Dear God, shield me from connections that drain my energy and lead me astray. Help me recognize and distance myself from those who spread negativity and hatred.

4. Heavenly Father, I pray for companions who reflect your love, kindness, and humility. Surround me with those who uplift my spirit and encourage my growth.

5. Lord, grant me discernment in choosing the souls I allow into my life. Help me seek out safe and nurturing connections that enrich my journey.

6. God, guide me to invest my energy in pursuits that yield positive returns. May every interaction and endeavor contribute to my growth and well-being.

7. Merciful Father, remind me to prioritize rest and recharge. Grant me peaceful sleep and moments of self-care that rejuvenate my body, mind, and spirit.

8. Lord, give me the strength to set healthy boundaries in my relationships and commitments. Help me allocate my time wisely and honor my own needs.

9. Holy Spirit fill me with your love, peace, and joy. Equip me to pour out blessings onto others from an overflow of your presence in my life.

10. Heavenly Father, guide my steps as I navigate the challenges of this world. Grant me the wisdom to make the best use of my time, walking in your light and purpose.

Reflect

# 3

# Minding Your Business Is Free

What are you a part of? Whose conversations do you join? Have you ever found yourself in places where you weren't invited? Remember, it's best not to go if you're not invited. And if you're not asked to join certain talks, it's better not to get involved. You might be wondering what I mean by all this. Well, I'm talking about the importance of minding your own business.

Minding your business is like a special gift from God, and the best part is that it doesn't cost anything. Some of us really like helping others, and that's a great thing. But sometimes, we try to help or get involved even when not needed or welcomed. It's like trying to fix something that isn't broken or occupying spaces where you are not welcomed. We have to take a moment and think about ourselves. It's not always a good idea to be too involved in things that don't concern us. Make yourself available and wait for an invitation.

Do you sometimes find yourself trying to fix everyone else's problems? Do you tell them what to do and how to do it, thinking you have all the answers? If that sounds like you, it's time to stop and think. Remember, you also have yourself to take care of. It's important to focus on your own needs and help others when they ask for it and when you can. Remember obedience is better than sacrifice. Learn to lean on the Holy Spirit when it comes to you and others as well.

When you focus on your business, you're making yourself stronger. You're learning to love and care for yourself, and that's the first step to being able to help others. Being too busy with things that don't concern you can lead to gossiping and wasting energy. Just like it says in 1 Timothy 5:13, some people waste time going from one place to another, discussing things they shouldn't be discussing.

But we can do better. Listening to gossip or unnecessary talk can waste your precious time. Your time is valuable, so don't waste it. Instead, use it wisely by focusing on what truly matters to you. Minding your own business doesn't cost anything; it can make you a better person and a great help to others.

Stay focused on your own path, and remember your job is to make yourself available, and if someone needs you, they'll ask for your help. If they want you in their life, they'll invite you. Love yourself first, and that will help you love others even better. Stay away from things that don't concern you and work on becoming the best version of yourself. By focusing on yourself, you can also help others rise up. Let the foundation of minding your own business be love.

Love embodies patience and kindness; it's far removed from engaging in idle gossip. Therefore, before immersing yourself in any endeavor, take a moment to pause, assess your own schedule, and communicate your availability and capabilities upfront. If you choose to participate, ensure you possess the necessary time and energy, and confirm that your assistance is genuinely welcome.

Take care of yourself, improve your weaknesses, practice self-discipline, and avoid being too busy with things that don't matter. If we all learn to mind our business, we can improve things. Remember, minding your business is a gift from God, and it's absolutely free. May God bless you in all that you do.

**Scriptures:**

Proverbs 17:28:
*"Even a fool is counted wise when he holds his peace; when he shuts his lips, he is considered perceptive."*

1 Thessalonians 4:11:
*"that you also aspire to lead a quiet life, to mind your own business, and to work with your own hands, as we commanded you,"*

Galatians 6:4-5:
*"But let each one examine his own work, and then he will have rejoicing in himself alone, and not in another. For each one shall bear his own load."*

1 Timothy 5:13:
*"And besides they learn to be idle, wandering about from house to house, and not only idle but also gossips and busybodies, saying things which they ought not."*

James 1:19:
*"So then, my beloved brethren, let every man be swift*

*to hear, slow to speak, slow to wrath;"*

Proverbs 20:3:

*"It is honorable for a man to stop striving, since any fool can start a quarrel."*

Matthew 7:3-5:

*"And why do you look at the speck in your brother's eye, but do not consider the plank in your own eye? Or how can you say to your brother, 'Let me remove the speck from your eye'; and look, a plank is in your own eye? Hypocrite! First remove the plank from your own eye, and then you will see clearly to remove the speck from your brother's eye."*

Proverbs 25:17:

*"Seldom set foot in your neighbor's house, lest he become weary of you and hate you."*

Romans 12:18:

*"If it is possible, as much as depends on you, live peaceably with all men."*

Proverbs 26:17:

*"He who passes by and meddles in a quarrel not his own is like one who takes a dog by the ears."*

## Prayer Points:

1. Heavenly Father, I am grateful for your guidance in helping me discern where I should be, what conversations I should engage in, and where my focus should lie.

2. Lord, grant me wisdom to recognize the importance of minding my own business. Help me resist the urge to get involved where I am not needed.

3. Dear God, help me take moments to reflect on my actions and intentions. Guide me to examine whether I am too involved in matters that don't concern me.

4. Heavenly Father, as I focus on my own business, may I find strength in self-care. Teach me to love and care for myself, so I can be a source of support for others.

5. Lord, shield me from the temptation of gossip and un-necessary talk. Help me use my words to build up and encourage, rather than waste energy on negativity.

6. Dear God, help me learn to set healthy boundaries with love. May I focus on my own journey while being open to helping others when asked and needed.

7. Heavenly Father instills in me patience and kindness. May my interactions be characterized by love and understand-ing, rather than rushed judgments.

8. Lord, grant me discernment to know when to step back and when to get involved. Help me avoid unnecessary commitments that drain my time and energy.

9. Dear God, grant me the courage to prioritize what truly matters. Help me focus on my own growth and well-being, as I strive to be a better version of myself.

10. Heavenly Father, I thank you for the gift of minding my own business. May I use this gift to spread love, make positive changes, and glorify you in all that I do. Amen.

Reflect

4

# Boundaries Unleashed: Nurturing Divine Balance

I was stressed out, overwhelmed, and always running around, but I didn't feel I was getting anything done. It was a confusing time for me. I prayed for long hours but did not feel Jesus's presence, did not sleep well, and did not eat properly. I didn't have time for my family, husband, or kids. I was helping everyone, but I felt so lonely and tired. But the worst part was I wasn't even helping myself. Something just didn't feel right, so I decided to go back to the source and learn about Jesus' life when He was on Earth as a human.

With the help of God's Spirit, I connected with different mentors and people who showed me a new way to look at the Bible. This gave me the courage to really study the Word of God and Jesus' life. Yes, Jesus was God, the powerful Creator, but He also became a human like us. Matthew 28:17 says that when people saw Him, some worshipped Him, but others doubted Him. It was because He looked just like them – just like you and me at some point in His life.

As I started reading the Bible with this new perspective, I fell more in love with Jesus. He loves us so much that He sent His only Son to die for us. Jesus went through real pain, even on the cross. They nailed His hands and feet, and it must have been excruciating. Jesus felt pain and anger, just like we do. There were times He even cried.

I learned that it's okay to cry and feel things deeply. Jesus showed us that by weeping in the Bible. He also taught us about healthy boundaries. He said "no" to people who wanted to use Him or manipulate Him. He didn't hang out with those who were proud or treated Him badly. Jesus knew when to say "no," and that's good.

Luke 5:15-16 says that even though people wanted to see Jesus and be healed by Him, He often went to lonely places to pray. He knew when to take time for Himself and connect with God. This made me realize that I need to set healthy boundaries, too. I can't help everyone all the time. I need to take care of myself and recharge with God.

I also saw that Jesus fought for what was right. When people were against Him, He stood up for Himself and went His own way. He showed us that we don't have to accept mistreatment or bad behavior from others.

Looking at Jesus' life, I saw He rested when He needed to rest, cried when He needed to cry, and rejoiced when He was happy. He healed people and worked hard when it was time. I realized that I wasn't relying on God enough for my needs and helping others. I was trying to do everything independently, which made me stressed and overwhelmed.

Learning from Jesus, I saw that setting healthy boundaries is important. It's like a good friend that helps you. I learned to love myself by setting boundaries the way Jesus did. Remember, I am not my own – my body, mind, and soul belong to God. To set boundaries for yourself, you must be aware of your needs. Let Jesus guide you and learn to love yourself by setting boundaries like He did.

**Scriptures:**

Psalm 23:2-3:

*"He makes me to lie down in green pastures; He leads me beside the still waters. He restores my soul; He leads me in the paths of righteousness for His name's sake."*

Matthew 11:28-30:

*"Come to Me, all you who labor and are heavy laden, and I will give you rest. Take My yoke upon you and learn from Me, for I am gentle and lowly in heart, and you will find rest for your souls. For My yoke is easy and My burden is light."*

Ecclesiastes 3:1:

*"To everything there is a season, a time for every purpose under heaven."*

1 Corinthians 6:19-20:

*"Or do you not know that your body is the temple of the Holy Spirit who is in you, whom you have from God, and you are not your own? For you were bought at a price; therefore glorify God in your body and in your spirit, which are God's."*

Philippians 4:6-7:

*"Be anxious for nothing, but in everything by prayer and supplication, with thanksgiving, let your requests be made known to God; and the peace of God, which surpasses all understanding, will guard your hearts and minds through Christ Jesus."*

Galatians 6:9:
*"And let us not grow weary while doing good, for in due season we shall reap if we do not lose heart."*

Proverbs 16:3:
*"Commit your works to the Lord, and your thoughts will be established."*

Matthew 6:33:
*"But seek first the kingdom of God and His righteousness, and all these things shall be added to you."*

1 Peter 5:7:
*"Casting all your care upon Him, for He cares for you."*

Psalm 46:10:
*"Be still, and know that I am God; I will be exalted among the nations, I will be exalted in the earth."*

**Prayer Points:**

1. Heavenly Father, in times of stress and overwhelm, help me to remember that You are my refuge and strength.

Teach me to find rest in Your presence and to trust in Your perfect plan for my life.

2. Lord, grant me wisdom to balance my responsibilities and commitments. Help me recognize when I'm spreading myself too thin and guide me in making choices that align with Your will.

3. Dear God, show me how to prioritize my family amidst the busyness of life. Grant me the ability to nurture and cherish the relationships that matter most to me.

4. Jesus, my Savior, as I learn from Your life on Earth, help me to see You as both divine and human. May Your example inspire me to approach life's challenges with grace and resilience.

5. Heavenly Father, teach me that it's okay to show vulnerability, just as Jesus did. May I find strength in admitting my struggles and seeking Your comfort in times of pain.

6. Lord, guide me in setting healthy boundaries in my life. Help me to say "no" when needed and to recognize the value of self-care for my well-being.

7. Compassionate God grant me the courage to embrace my emotions and seek healing. Just as Jesus wept, remind me that it's alright to express my feelings and find solace in Your presence.

8. Heavenly Father, help me discern relationships that align with Your purpose for me. May I be surrounded by those who uplift and encourage me, just as Jesus chose His companions wisely.

9. Lord Jesus, as I see how You withdrew to lonely places to pray, guide me in carving out moments of solitude to connect with You. Strengthen our relationship through these intimate conversations.

10. Loving God, I surrender my tendency to rely solely on myself. Teach me to trust Your provision and guidance, knowing that You have a purpose for my life that goes beyond my understanding.

Reflect

# 5

# Soul's Sanctuary: Discovering God's Presence

L ife is like a big puzzle, filled with important pieces we need to fit together. We eat, work, sleep, and make time for other things that matter to us. Have you ever thought about how we decide what to do first, second, or third? It's like making a list of what's most important to us. This list can get pretty long because there are so many things we feel we need to do in our lives.

But here's something to remember: no matter how long our list is, we all have the same amount of time in a day—24 hours. Time is like a gift that we can't add more of. We can rearrange our list and change things around, but time stays the same. It's like a constant friend that never changes. Have you ever thought about how you use your time wisely?

In our world today, many things can distract us. We must catch up on things, join in activities, and meet society's demands. But among all this, it's vital to find where God fits into our lives. Having God with us feels amazing. It's like having a special friendship with Jesus. It's great to say that we know

Him.

Our primary focus should be on nurturing our friendship with Jesus. Yet, in doing so, it's equally important to consider how Jesus would guide us in forming relationships with others, including siblings, friends, parents, mentors, and beyond. Sometimes, we inadvertently place God further down our priority list, perhaps at number 20, 30, or even 100. However, I encourage you to take up the challenge of placing God first. Let His presence be akin to a radiant star placed right at the pinnacle of your list.

The Bible teaches us this in Proverbs 16:3: *"Trust in the Lord with all your heart and lean not on your own understanding; in all your ways submit to Him, and He will make your paths straight."* This means that everything else falls into place when we put God first. It's like creating a beautiful picture where God is at the center.

Did you know it's easy to accidentally put other things before God? Good things, like work or money, can become more important than God. Sometimes, we don't even realize it's happening. That's why it's important to consider where God stands on our list. We can't have two most important things – we have to choose.

The Bible tells us in Matthew 6:25, *"No one can serve two masters. Either you will hate and love the other or be devoted to the one and despise the other."* You can't serve God and something else at the same time. You can't make God and something else first—it doesn't work. So, where does God stand in your life?

I want you to stop momentarily and think about this: Where does God fit on your list? Is He there as a friend, or is He the very first? If you can, I challenge you to pray and think about it. Make Jesus your top priority. How can you do that? Just like you spend time with a friend, spend time with Jesus. Learn about Him and let Him guide you.

I've gained insight into the role God occupies in my life. I assess various aspects such as finances, my children, and my career to gauge where God's presence fits in. Occasionally, I group these elements together to determine their priority. Placing God as the foremost priority in every aspect can be challenging, particularly when it comes to areas like finances and other commitments. I propose the idea of categorizing these aspects to better comprehend where God's significance lies within each of them. Remember, Jesus doesn't solely claim the top position; He is also deeply concerned about every item on your list. His care and compassion extend to all. As you place Him at the forefront, it signifies your surrender to Him, inviting His influence to encompass your entire list, from the highest to the lowest priority.

So, I challenge you today to make sure God comes first. Make having a relationship with Jesus your top priority. I believe that when you do, you'll see amazing results. Remember, God loves you and wants the best for you.

**Scriptures:**

Psalm 90:12:
*"So teach us to number our days, that we may gain a heart of wisdom."*

Ephesians 5:15-16:
*"See then that you walk circumspectly, not as fools but as wise, redeeming the time, because the days are evil."*

Colossians 3:2:

*"Set your mind on things above, not on things on the earth."*

Psalm 37:5:

*"Commit your way to the Lord, trust also in Him, and He shall bring it to pass."*

Psalm 139:16:

*"Your eyes saw my substance, being yet unformed. And in Your book they all were written, the days fashioned for me, when as yet there were none of them."*

Matthew 6:33:

*"But seek first the kingdom of God and His righteousness, and all these things shall be added to you."*

Proverbs 3:5-6:

*"Trust in the Lord with all your heart, and lean not on your own understanding; in all your ways acknowledge Him, and He shall direct your paths."*

James 4:14:

*"Whereas you do not know what will happen tomorrow. For what is your life? It is even a vapor that appears for a little time and then vanishes away."*

Psalm 46:10:

*"Be still, and know that I am God; I will be exalted among the nations, I will be exalted in the earth."*

Psalm 16:11:

*"You will show me the path of life; in Your presence is fullness of joy; at Your right hand are pleasures forevermore."*

**Prayer Points:**

1. Heavenly Father, I'm grateful for the intricate puzzle of life that You've woven for me. Grant me the wisdom to understand each piece and to live purposefully according to Your plan.
2. Lord, as I make decisions, guide me to discern what truly matters in my life, aligning my choices with Your divine will.
3. Father, please teach me to manage my time wisely, recognizing the significance of each day as a precious gift from You. May I use it to bring glory to Your name.
4. Dear God, help me arrange my priorities like pieces of a puzzle, so that my time is well-spent and every endeavor honors You.
5. Gracious Lord, amidst the busyness and distractions, show me where You perfectly fit in – right at the center of my life.
6. Lord Jesus, may my relationship with You shine as the brightest star atop my list, overshadowing any other concerns that vie for my attention.
7. Heavenly Father, I place my complete trust in You, knowing that when You hold the primary place in my heart, my path becomes clear and purposeful.
8. Lord, reveal to me any areas where I inadvertently place

other things before You. Grant me the wisdom and insight to choose You above all else.

9. Dear God, as I reflect on my life, I acknowledge that You deserve the central place in my heart and my daily activities. Guide me to align my life accordingly.

10. Gracious Father, as I spend time nurturing my friendship with Jesus, strengthen our bond. Help me to put You above all else, and in doing so, may I experience the abundance of Your blessings.

Reflect

6

# The Journey Inward: A Dance of Self-Love

Who holds a place in your heart? Consider the love most mothers, for instance, have for their children—a love demonstrated through devoted care and nurturing. They ensure their children's well-being in body, mind, soul, and emotions. This includes providing proper nourishment, monitoring developmental milestones, and fostering physical fitness for their activities. They accompany them to medical appointments, pray, and teach them about faith. They address emotional needs, comforting them when they cry, and inquiring about their troubles. The mother's joy is often bound to the child's happiness. Happiness is commonly said to be a state of mind and a significant choice.

Yet, we should extend this kind of love to ourselves. Just as we invest in the happiness of our loved ones, we should prioritize our own well-being. Understanding oneself, being truthful, and embracing one's journey in self-love is vital. Just as you believe that God created those you care about, recognize that you are wonderfully crafted by His hands. You are equally deserving of love and investment.

The Bible reminds us that we are fearfully and wonderfully made, encompassing everyone—including yourself. As God took His time to create you, you must also devote time to self-investment. This journey involves caring for your body, mind, spirit, and emotions, all God-given gifts. To attain balance, you might excel in one area more than another. Regardless, commit to persistently loving and nurturing yourself.

Challenge the misconceptions you hold about yourself. Examine past traumas and negative experiences that may hinder self-love. Visualize yourself at moments of neglect or when love was lacking. Recognize how these experiences may have shaped your core values and affected your self-esteem.

Remember that self-love is an ongoing endeavor. Life changes, people change, but you must continually remind yourself to love who you are. Like the constant care a child requires, apply that attention to yourself. Pause when needed, but always prioritize self-love.

One crucial aspect is cultivating a relationship with yourself. You build connections with others at work, church or with family. Yet, how often do you invest in your relationship with yourself? When did you last spend quality time alone or engage in self-reflection? When did you last ask yourself how you felt or treated yourself to something special?

Loving yourself is a full-time commitment. Remember, perfection isn't attainable—a trait unique to Jesus Christ. Regular self-attention ensures you can love yourself fully and, in turn, bless others with your positivity and vitality.

**Scriptures:**

Psalm 139:13-14:

*"For You formed my inward parts; You covered me in my mother's womb. I will praise You, for I am fearfully and wonderfully made; marvelous are Your works, and that my soul knows very well."*

Isaiah 49:15:

*"Can a woman forget her nursing child, and not have compassion on the son of her womb?  Surely they may forget, yet I will not forget you."*

Ephesians 2:10:

*"For we are His workmanship, created in Christ Jesus for good works, which God prepared beforehand that we should walk in them."*

Matthew 22:37-39:

*"Jesus said to him, 'You shall love the Lord your God with all your heart, with all your soul, and with all your mind.'  This is the first and great commandment.  And the second is like it:  'You shall love your neighbor as yourself.'"*

Psalm 46:10:

*"Be still, and know that I am God; I will be exalted among the nations, I will be exalted in the earth."*

Romans 12:3:

*"For I say, through the grace given to me, to everyone*

*who is among you, not to think of himself more highly than he ought to think, but to think soberly, as God has dealt to each one a measure of faith."*

1 Corinthians 6:19-20:
*"Or do you not know that your body is the temple of the Holy Spirit who is in you, whom you have from God, and you are not your own?  For you were bought at a price; therefore glorify God in your body and in your spirit, which are God's."*

Proverbs 4:23:
*"Keep your heart with all diligence, for out of it spring the issues of life."*

Galatians 6:4-5:
*"But let each one examine his own work, and then he will have rejoicing in himself alone, and not in another. For each one shall bear his own load."*

Philippians 4:13:
*"I can do all things through Christ who strengthens me."*

**Prayer Points:**

1. Dear Heavenly Father, in the sacred moments of reflection, guide me into the depths of my heart. Just as a mother's love nurtures, help me embrace your love that knows no

bounds. Remind me that just as mothers care for their children, I am worthy of self-love and care. Grant me the strength to invest in my own being as You have crafted me. Amen.

2. Gracious God, Creator of all, helps me see the beauty in each being, including myself. Let the winds of Your whispers remind me that I am fearfully and wonderfully made. Just as You sculpted us with care, empower me to invest in my body, mind, and spirit. May I live as a testament to Your craftsmanship. Amen.

3. Loving God, in the journey to love myself, guide me through the depths of my being. As mothers guide their young, lead me toward the warmth of my own embrace. Let me pause to ask, "How am I?" and shower myself with kindness. Give me strength to embrace my weaknesses and seek balance in body, mind, and spirit. Amen.

4. Heavenly Father, as I delve deep into the tapestry of my past, illuminate the shadows that haunt me. Just as mothers address their children's needs, help me confront the pains of yesteryear. Grant me the courage to release chains that hinder my self-love. In Your light, may I find healing and growth. Amen.

5. Gracious God, in a world of change, be my steady anchor. As mothers care for their young around the clock, remind me to nurture myself with unwavering devotion. May I find solace in Your presence, knowing that my journey is woven by Your hands. Grant me resilience to stay committed to self-love. Amen.

6. Loving Creator, help me build a sacred bond with myself as I do with others. Just as relationships flourish through time spent together, guide me to sit with my soul and con-

verse with my inner being. Grant me the grace to extend kindness and reassurance to myself. In this devotion, may I find strength. Amen.

7. Dear Lord, I humbly acknowledge that no human is flawless, but perfection resides in You alone. As mothers nurture their children's growth, remind me that acknowledging my imperfections is a step towards Your grace. May I learn from my mistakes and grow stronger in Your love. Amen.

8. Heavenly Father, as stars follow the night, may my heart's garden flourish with self-love. Just as a vessel carries life's blessings, empower me to nurture myself, so I may bless others abundantly. Grant me the wisdom to care for my own heart, so that I may overflow with love for those around me. Amen.

9. Loving God, in the intricate journey of self-love, remind me that grace is found in embracing imperfection. As Christ's perfection shines, teach me to embrace my own journey with compassion. May I draw strength from You as I navigate the path of self-discovery and growth. Amen.

10. Dear Heavenly Father, in the tapestry of life, help me embrace the love You hold for me. Just as mothers care for their children, let me bask in the depths of Your love. As I learn to love myself, guide me to be a vessel of love, blessing others with the overflow of Your grace. Amen.

Reflect

# 7

# Triumphing Beyond Men: Trusting God's Plan

Have you ever felt the weight of your mistakes, the pain of making someone cry, or the ache of letting others down? Have you gone to bed with a heavy heart, burdened by wrong decisions? These moments remind us that we are human, crafted from fragile flesh, and our core nature bears the stain of sin. Sin has woven itself into our very being, tainting our thoughts and actions, causing us to stumble and hurt those around us.

The truth is, people will let us down, just as we will let them down. Think of times when someone's actions wounded your soul, or their promises were broken, leaving you disappointed. Our sinful nature casts shadows on our relationships, reminding us of our imperfections. This is why placing our trust in humanity alone is a fragile endeavor.

The Scriptures tell us in Romans 3:23, *"For all have sinned and fallen short of the glory of God."* This humbling truth calls us to recognize our limitations and the reality of our fallen nature. It's crucial to ponder where we anchor our trust and find our refuge. Who truly deserves our trust? How can we discern this?

Do not place your unwavering trust solely in mortal beings—siblings, friends, even yourself—because they cannot ultimately save you. While they can be instruments of help and support, they are not infallible. They do not hold the keys to your destiny or determine your success. To find unshakable trust, turn your gaze to the Creator of the heavens and the earth. The One who intricately designed everything, including you, remains steadfast. He is a God who is forever faithful and never failing.

Even in our love for others, it's important to distinguish between love and trust. The Bible encourages us to love even our enemies, but trust is a different m atter. Understand that loving someone doesn't guarantee they won't hurt us. Love does not build an impenetrable shield against disappointment. Trusting yourself is another avenue that can lead to vulnerability. Instead, direct your trust toward the God residing within you. Lean on Him in times of decision-making, seeking His guidance and wisdom.

In times of trouble or uncertainty, remember to lean on God. Turn your heart towards the spiritual and discover that everything else may falter, but God remains unchanging. Amid the shifting sands of life, His faithfulness stands tall. It may seem unusual, but both you and others may stumble and falter. The beauty lies in the fact that God never falters. He is consistently loving, unswervingly caring, and eternally dependable. He stands sovereign and unfailing, an unbreakable rock upon which you can build your trust.

**Scriptures:**

Romans 3:23:

*"For all have sinned and fall short of the glory of God."*

Psalm 51:5:

*"Behold, I was brought forth in iniquity, and in sin my mother conceived me."*

Psalm 103:14:

*"For He knows our frame; He remembers that we are dust."*

Psalm 38:4:

*"For my iniquities have gone over my head; like a heavy burden, they are too heavy for me."*

Proverbs 3:5-6:

*"Trust in the Lord with all your heart, and lean not on your own understanding; in all your ways acknowledge Him, and He shall direct your paths."*

Psalm 118:8:

*"It is better to trust in the Lord than to put confidence in man."*

Jeremiah 17:5:

*"Thus says the Lord: 'Cursed is the man who trusts in man and makes flesh his strength, whose heart departs from the Lord.'"*

Psalm 146:3-5:

*"Do not put your trust in princes, nor in a son of man, in whom there is no help. His spirit departs, he returns to his earth; in that very day his plans perish. Happy is he who has the God of Jacob for his help, whose hope is in the Lord his God."*

Psalm 62:8:

*"Trust in Him at all times, you people; pour out your heart before Him; God is a refuge for us."*

Isaiah 26:4:

*"Trust in the Lord forever, for in Yah, the Lord, is everlasting strength."*

**Prayer Points:**

1. Dear Heavenly Father, I come before You with a heavy heart, acknowledging the weight of my mistakes. I have caused pain, and I've let others down. Please forgive me for my shortcomings. Help me learn from my errors and strive to be better.

2. Loving God, when my actions have made others cry and my decisions have hurt them, I pray for their healing. Ease their pain and bring comfort to their hearts. May Your love mend the wounds I've unintentionally caused.

3. Lord, I have faced the ache of wrong decisions, and I'm burdened by them. Grant me clarity and wisdom in my choices. Guide me on the path that aligns with Your will,

so I may avoid repeating my mistakes.

4. Heavenly Father, I am human, made from fragile flesh and prone to sin. Help me to accept my imperfections and lean on Your grace. Thank You for loving me despite my flaws.

5. Lord, I've experienced disappointment when others have let me down. Teach me to trust wisely, to recognize that human nature is imperfect. Guide me in discerning where to place my trust and whom to rely on.

6. Dear God, in a world of shifting relationships, I find solace in You. Your Word reminds me that all have sinned and fallen short, but Your love remains constant. Be my refuge, my unchanging anchor.

7. Heavenly Father, help me discern where to anchor my trust. Remind me that mortal beings, even those I love, cannot ultimately save me. Direct my gaze to You, the Creator of all things, who is steadfast and unwavering.

8. Loving God, help me differentiate between love and trust. While love may not shield me from disappointment, guide me in placing my unwavering trust in You. May I lean on Your wisdom and understanding.

9. Lord, I humbly admit that even trusting myself can lead to vulnerability. Instead, I place my trust in Your unchanging nature. Amidst life's uncertainties, You remain faithful and dependable. Strengthen my faith in Your constant love.

10. Heavenly Father, may Your blessings encompass me as I find solace and strength in Your unwavering love and faithfulness. Through the trials of life, may I stand firm on the rock of Your unbreakable love. In Your name, I pray. Amen.

## Reflect

# 8

# Embracing Your Unique Journey

Once, I gathered my courage to ask my dad about my birth story. With a gentle smile, he shared a tale that held history and emotions. *"Your mom left you with your grandmother,"* he said, *"and I had the option to journey and find you there."* These words held the story of my origin - a tale of hope, discovery, and destiny's whispers.

Entering the world, I learned I was a "girl," the fourth daughter in our lineage. This fact seemed simple, but beneath it lay a layer of sadness. Four daughters in a row brought unmet hopes and sorrow. It cast a shadow on my parents and our family. I often wondered about their feelings when they heard another girl had arrived.

In my childhood, a significant moment came when my parents considered entrusting me to my aunt. Fate took a different turn, and I remained part of my family. My aunt's refusal puzzled me. So, one day, I gathered the courage to ask my dad about it.

Being the fourth girl and child, I felt differences in treatment that left me feeling out of place. I grappled with these feelings and sought understanding. Talking to my father uncovered another chapter: in my teenage years, I was cared for by another aunt, becoming like a second mother. This discovery made me explore my family connections.

Expressing the pain of feeling overlooked isn't easy. I remember mixing laughter and somber truth the first time I talked about it. This mix made me confront my pain directly, addressing the hidden wounds beneath the surface.

Growing up, I wrestled with trust, belonging, and the emotions these struggles brought. In my heart, anger, and solitude coexisted. I delved into these feelings through introspection. Have you ever revisited a memory and found new layers of emotion? It's like looking at a familiar painting and seeing new shades.

Hope shines through Jesus, a constant friend and guide. He's a presence beyond isolation, offering unwavering companionship. My relationship with my parents grew deeper as we understood each other better. The embrace of a father's love, crafted with divine care, reaffirms my value. I realized that our flaws, mistakes, and the wrongs against us don't define us. God's grace reminds us of our worth and guides us to self-acceptance.

An old story of Samuel choosing a king teaches that appearances are deceiving. God looks at our hearts, not surface traits. This story resonates with my journey. Like young David becoming a king, we find strength in God's love, defying expectations.

In life's intricate tapestry, our uniqueness shines. Just as David became a king with God's help, we discover strength and worth in God's love. This constant presence assures us that our origin, appearance, and experiences contribute to our purpose and value.

**Scriptures:**

Proverbs 18:16:
*"A man's gift makes room for him and brings him before great men."*

1 Corinthians 12:7:
*"But the manifestation of the Spirit is given to each one for the profit of all."*

Romans 12:6:
*"Having then gifts differing according to the grace that is given to us."*

Ephesians 2:10:
*"For we are His workmanship, created in Christ Jesus for good works, which God prepared beforehand that we should walk in them."*

Matthew 25:14-15:
*"For the kingdom of heaven is like a man traveling to a far country, who called his own servants and delivered his goods to them. And to one, he gave five talents, to another two, and to another one, to each according to his own ability."*

1 Peter 4:10:
*"As each one has received a gift, minister it to one*

*another, as good stewards of the manifold grace of God."*

Colossians 3:23-24:

*"And whatever you do, do it heartily, as to the Lord and not to men, knowing that from the Lord you will receive the reward of the inheritance; for you serve the Lord Christ."*

Romans 8:28:

*"And we know that all things work together for good to those who love God, to those who are the called according to His purpose."*

Psalm 139:13-14:

*"For You formed my inward parts; You covered me in my mother's womb. I will praise You, for I am fearfully and wonderfully made; marvelous are Your works, and that my soul knows very well."*

2 Timothy 1:6:

*"Therefore I remind you to stir up the gift of God which is in you through the laying on of my hands."*

**Prayer Points:**

1. Heavenly Father, grant me the courage to seek understanding and ask the difficult questions, just as I did when I inquired about my origin. May I find strength in vulnerability and the wisdom to face the past with an open

heart.

2. Lord, help me embrace the unique identity You've bestowed upon me. Though the world may cast shadows of disappointment, let me remember that Your purpose for me is perfect and meaningful.

3. Gracious God, guide me in understanding the intricate threads of family connections. May I appreciate the twists and turns that have led me to where I am today, and find beauty in the complexity of relationships.

4. Merciful Father, I lay before You the wounds of feeling overlooked and dismissed. Heal the ache that lies hidden beneath laughter's surface and grant me the strength to address and heal these hurts.

5. Lord, as I navigate the currents of life, help me uncover my purpose and belonging. Illuminate my path and guide me in using my unique gifts and experiences to make a positive impact in Your kingdom.

6. Jesus, my enduring companion and guide, I am grateful for Your unwavering presence in my life. Thank You for being my confidant, my friend, and my source of strength in times of isolation.

7. Heavenly Father, I thank You for crafting me with divine precision. Help me recognize that my worth is not defined by imperfections or transgressions, but by Your infinite love and grace.

8. Lord, grant me the discernment to look beyond appearances and judgments, just as You do. Help me see the hearts of others and appreciate the true essence that lies within each person.

9. Gracious God, as I navigate the challenges and complexities of life, empower me with the resilience to rise above

expectations and limitations.  Like David, let me find strength in Your unwavering love.

10. Heavenly Father, I thank You for weaving my story into the intricate tapestry of existence. May I always remember that my origins, experiences, and appearance contribute to a purpose greater than I can fathom. Help me recognize my inherent value in Your eyes.

## Reflect

9

# Trusting God's Plan Through Pain

Finally, a positive result! Gratitude poured forth – "Thank you, Jesus." I can vividly recall how I spent that entire day praising God. The joy that swelled within me felt almost magical. It was as though my heart was dancing with happiness. This was truly one of the most beautiful moments I had ever experienced. The long journey of waiting for countless negative results culminated in this positive news. We were expecting our first child. The elation was beyond words; we couldn't contain our joy.

Our excitement knew no bounds. We spread the news across the globe, calling family members from Europe, Africa, and the United States. Their voices echoed with genuine happiness; their well-wishes were like treasures. Every corner of the world was celebrating this wonderful blessing. But the day had even more in store. We decided to personally share the news with my sisters. I can still remember the exact spot where I sat, feeling the warmth of the room enveloping me. After spending time with my sisters, the anticipation became too much to bear. We had to share the incredible news that we were going to be parents. Their happiness echoed ours, filling the air with jubilant celebration.

Yet, a sudden shift occurred as the day continued, around 7 p.m.. Cramps began to grip me, and the joy I had felt earlier turned into an unsettling discomfort. Confusion and pain became my companions. I rushed to the bathroom, only to find spotting on my undergarment. Fear and uncertainty gripped me. Despite my background in healthcare, I couldn't piece together what was happening. Overwhelmed, I needed to leave, to retreat to the safety of my home, and maybe pretend none of it was happening. Tears streamed down my face as I prayed on the journey back. Each minute felt like an eternity as I wrestled with my deepest fears and the intensity of the physical pain.

Arriving home, I hurried to the shower, hoping to cleanse away the turmoil. But the pain intensified, and I found myself numb. My husband, with a tender heart, pulled me from the shower as the cramps and bleeding grew worse. And then, it hit me like a wave – a miscarriage. The day that began with pure happiness was now a torrent of confusion, fear, hurt, and shame.

In the middle of the night, it happened once more. There, in the toilet, was the embryo. It might be unsettling, but I couldn't let it go unnoticed. I held it, a small and fragile symbol of loss. After numerous prayers and countless tears a week later, I stood before God and released it. It was a painful farewell, and I admit I didn't know what to expect. I knelt before God, crying, and told Him I was giving my "Shalom" back to Him. This gift, so precious, so costly, had to be surrendered. It was hard – oh, so hard. But I needed to trust that God knew what was best. And more than that, I realized I could trust Him with every facet of my life – the joys, the hurts, the struggles, and the pain.

Remember, God doesn't only walk with us during the good times. He's there through the bad, the ugly, and the painful. Even in moments of shame, we must not turn away from Him, for He longs to bless us. The truth is, sometimes, our pain doesn't make sense. But one thing is certain – Jesus is in control, and nothing surprises Him. Think of your most cherished gift and offer it to Him, knowing He can transform it for your good.

Let's consider the story of the woman with the alabaster flask in Matthew 26:6-13. This story teaches us that God values our heart's intent, even when others may not understand. The woman's extravagant gift was questioned by some, but Jesus saw the depth of her love. Similarly, amid our pain and loss, God sees our hearts and the sacrifices we make. Our stories, like hers, are treasured by God.

**Scriptures:**

Psalm 28:7:
*"The Lord is my strength and my shield; my heart trusted in Him, and I am helped; therefore my heart greatly rejoices, and with my song, I will praise Him."*

1 Thessalonians 5:16-18:
*"Rejoice always, pray without ceasing, in everything give thanks; for this is the will of God in Christ Jesus for you."*

Psalm 34:18:
*"The Lord is near to those who have a broken heart and saves such as have a contrite spirit."*

Isaiah 41:10:

*"Fear not, for I am with you; be not dismayed, for I am your God. I will strengthen you, yes, I will help you, I will uphold you with My righteous right hand."*

Romans 8:28:

*"And we know that all things work together for good to those who love God, to those who are the called according to His purpose."*

2 Corinthians 1:3-4:

*"Blessed be the God and Father of our Lord Jesus Christ, the Father of mercies and God of all comfort, who comforts us in all our tribulation, that we may be able to comfort those who are in any trouble, with the comfort with which we ourselves are comforted by God."*

Psalm 30:5:

*"For His anger is but for a moment, His favor is for life; weeping may endure for a night, but joy comes in the morning."*

Jeremiah 29:11:

*"For I know the thoughts that I think toward you, says the Lord, thoughts of peace and not of evil, to give you a future and a hope."*

James 1:2-4:

*"My brethren, count it all joy when you fall into various trials, knowing that the testing of your faith produces*

*patience. But let patience have its perfect work, that you may be perfect and complete, lacking nothing."*

Psalm 139:16:
  *"Your eyes saw my substance, being yet unformed. And in Your book they all were written, the days fashioned for me, when as yet there were none of them."*

**Prayer Points:**

1. Gracious God, thank you for the gift of positive news after waiting and hoping.  Today, I lift my heart in gratitude, knowing that You've turned my sorrow into joy.  Thank you, Jesus, for this beautiful moment.
2. Heavenly Father, as I reflect on the happiness that filled my heart, I'm reminded of Your unwavering love.  May this memory always inspire me to praise and dance in Your presence.
3. Lord, I lay before You the joy of our expectation. Bless and protect this new life growing within me. May Your grace and love surround our family as we await the arrival of our precious child.
4. Compassionate God, I lift up the pain of unexpected loss.  Hold me close in times of hurt and confusion.  Heal my wounds and grant me the strength to move forward with hope.
5. Lord, I place before You the fragility of life, represented by the embryo I held in my hand. Help me surrender all that I hold dear into Your loving care, knowing that You can turn

my losses into gains.

6. Almighty God, in moments of darkness, I trust that You're the light that guides me. I surrender my fears, hurts, and struggles into Your hands, for I know that You work all things for good.

7. Father, as I face moments of shame and uncertainty, remind me that Your love never wavers. Be with me in my pain and bless me with Your presence, for You are my refuge and strength.

8. God of wisdom, when life's puzzles don't make sense, grant me the patience to trust Your plan. Help me find meaning in moments of confusion, knowing that You hold the bigger picture.

9. Lord Jesus, just as You transformed the woman's gift into a memorial, transform my losses and sacrifices into offerings that honor You. May my story become a testament of Your grace.

10. Heavenly Father, I give You my heart, my joys, and my pain. May my life reflect the love and trust I have in You. Like the woman with the alabaster flask, may my intentions be a fragrant offering in Your sight.

Reflect

62

# 10

# Emerging From Emotional Scars to a Healthy Mental Health

Think about this: God gave us feelings, those big emotions like happiness, surprise, guilt, anger, love, joy, trust, and more. These feelings, like gifts from a loving father, are part of who we are. They help us make smart choices and have good relationships. And guess what? They even help us connect with God. So, those emotions matter a lot. It's important to understand them, to know why we're feeling what we feel. For instance, if you're mad, why? If you don't trust someone, what's making you feel that way? It might be because of where you are or the people around you. Understanding our feelings helps us be better people and make good choices, even when emotions run high.

You know what's tough? We live in a world where bad things can happen, people make mistakes, and things aren't always perfect. It's like an enemy is looking to cause trouble. But don't lose hope, because God's right there with us. He sent the Holy Spirit to guide us through life's ups and downs. Talking about feelings, when we let our feelings get twisted or misused, they can leave behind what I call "emotional scars." Those scars can mess up how we live and how God wants us to be free and happy. But here's the thing: we can heal even when feelings hurt us. We can't just ignore those scars; we need to figure out where they came from and fix it.

> Psalm 147:3 – *"He heals the brokenhearted and binds up their wounds."*

Let's talk about getting better. The first step is you. It's about taking charge of your life and understanding what's happening to you. Sure, you can ask for help, but you've got to start the journey. You've got to learn to help yourself first. And how? By putting in the effort. It's easy to want quick fixes, but healing those emotional scars takes time and some hard work. You've got to say, "Enough is enough," and work on yourself, even though it's tough. It's like planting a seed; it takes time for the plant to grow. So, as we decide it's time to heal, it's time to stop feeling bad. One practical thing you can do is write your thoughts down. Find a comfy spot, maybe get a nice drink, and write. You'll be surprised how it helps. Remember, you have the right to be at peace as a child of God. Doing this work won't just help you; it'll also help the people around you – your family, friends, and your community. You'll become a better version of yourself.

So, don't give up. You can break free from those emotional scars and feel better. It won't be easy, but it's possible. Many have done it before, and you can too. Remember, you've got the strength within you. Rise up, pick yourself up, and take control.

Let go of ignoring your feelings or just going along. Sit down, face those emotions, and work on healing. Invest in yourself, like building a strong house. When you do, you'll be able to use your feelings in ways that make God proud. So go ahead, rise above your hurt feelings, and step into a healthy, happy life. You're not alone – you've got this, and God's got you. In moments of emotional distress, remember the promises that sustain us. Romans 15:13 assures us of the unwavering support from the Lord. "May the God of hope fill you with all joy and peace in believing, so that by the power of the Holy Spirit you may abound in hope." Allow these words to resonate within you; they testify to the limitless wellspring of hope and strength. Even in the darkest times, believe in the power of this hope to uplift and heal. Embrace the joy and peace from faith, and know you are never alone in your struggles. The Holy Spirit guides and comforts you, enabling you to overcome adversity with resilience and optimism. As you navigate your journey, may this promise be a beacon of light, reminding you that you can flourish, even amidst challenges.

**Scriptures:**

Psalm 34:18:
*"The Lord is near to those who have a broken heart, and saves such as have a contrite spirit."*

Isaiah 41:10:
*"Fear not, for I am with you; be not dismayed, for I am your God. I will strengthen you, yes, I will help you, I will uphold you with My righteous right hand."*

Psalm 30:2:

"*O Lord my God, I cried out to You, and You healed me.*"

Jeremiah 29:11:

"*For I know the thoughts that I think toward you, says the Lord, thoughts of peace and not of evil, to give you a future and a hope.*"

Psalm 147:3:

"*He heals the brokenhearted and binds up their wounds.*"

Philippians 4:13:

"*I can do all things through Christ who strengthens me.*"

2 Corinthians 1:3-4:

"*Blessed be the God and Father of our Lord Jesus Christ, the Father of mercies and God of all comfort, who comforts us in all our tribulation.*"

Psalm 51:10:

"*Create in me a clean heart, O God, and renew a steadfast spirit within me.*"

Romans 8:37:

"*Yet in all these things we are more than conquerors through Him who loved us.*"

Isaiah 61:3:

*"To console those who mourn in Zion, to give them beauty for ashes, the oil of joy for mourning, the garment of praise for the spirit of heaviness."*

**Prayer Points:**

1. Heavenly Father, I come before You with gratitude for the gift of emotions.  Thank You for allowing me to experience a wide range of feelings that connect me with Your creation and purpose.  Help me understand and manage my emotions in ways that bring glory to You.

2. Lord, in a world marred by imperfections and difficulties, I seek Your guidance. When emotional scars threaten to hold me back, remind me that You are my refuge. Send Your Holy Spirit to heal and restore my heart, so I can find freedom and happiness in You.

3. Dear God, as I examine my feelings, grant me wisdom to discern the roots of my emotional wounds. Lead me to understand their sources and bring them into Your light for healing.  Psalm 147:3 assures me that You heal the brokenhearted; I trust in Your promise.

4. Heavenly Father, empower me to take charge of my journey towards emotional healing.  Grant me the strength to work on myself, even when it's difficult. Teach me to invest time and effort into my well-being, knowing that You are with me every step of the way.

5. Lord, when I face setbacks and challenges on this healing path, help me remember that my struggles are not in vain. Just as a seed grows into a strong plant, let me see

progress in my emotional growth. Grant me patience and perseverance.

6. God of Peace, I acknowledge my right to be at peace as Your child.  Grant me the courage to face my feelings and emotions head-on. May writing down my thoughts become a powerful tool in my journey to healing.

7. Loving Father, I lift up those around me who also stand to benefit from my healing journey. May the positive changes in my life inspire and impact those I love. Use my growth to encourage and support others on their paths to wellness.

8. Heavenly Father, when the weight of emotional scars seems overwhelming, remind me of the strength You have placed within me. Help me rise above my hurts, knowing that Your love and grace empower me to overcome.

9. Lord, I pray for the determination to break free from the shackles of emotional wounds. As I invest in myself, may I build a strong foundation for a healthier and happier life. May my actions reflect Your glory.

10. God of Hope, I hold onto Your promise from Romans 15:13. Fill me with Your joy and peace as I believe in Your power to transform my emotional scars into sources of strength. With Your Holy Spirit as my guide, I choose to abound in hope, knowing that You are by my side through every step of this journey.

Reflect

11

# Boundaries Are Your Friends

This chapter invites us to explore a profound idea–boundaries. Imagine boundaries as friendly guides, ready to journey alongside us. If you're not already friends with boundaries, it's time to make them your companions. Let's dive into this together.

Think about boundaries like the lines on a map that help us navigate. Picture what's under your control and what isn't. Things that fall outside your control include painful memories, actions of others, their opinions, and the traumas that weigh on your heart. These things, they're like a storm you can't stop. They've happened; you've met the people, been in the places, and faced what came your way. There's no going back to changing it. But here's the amazing part – you can control something, and that's your boundaries. You get to decide what enters and leaves your life, what gets a "yes" and what gets a "no." You're the gatekeeper of your energy, thoughts, choices, and actions. That's where your power lies.

In our world today, it's tough. Hurt and hardships can isolate us, and darkness creeps in. That's why caring for our minds is vital as we journey toward self-love, the kind Christ desires. Boundaries, from a biblical view, connect to self-control. It's about aligning your actions with your decisions, all guided by your inner self-control. It's not about controlling others; it's about mastering yourself. Remember, take a moment, and think about why you set each boundary. As you read on, consider going on a "date" with yourself. It's not about fancy places; it's about dedicating time for yourself. Write down your boundaries, examine them, and develop a list that will be your guide. Think of it like a mission statement just for you. Boundaries can be tailored to different situations, people, or places. They're like your armor, guarding against distractions. They're a way to set limits when challenges come knocking.

Boundaries appear everywhere – with friends, family, relationships, faith, and more. Sometimes saying "no" might feel wrong, but it's not. In Ephesians 4:15, the Bible speaks about speaking truth with love, helping us grow in Christ. It also talks about being honest with your "yes" and "no." So, before you answer, pause, and check your boundaries. Boundaries are friends who guide you to authentic connections. They help you love yourself so you can love others better.

Now, think about Jesus. He even took breaks when needed. He teaches us that it's okay to rest. So, remember, boundaries are your allies. Learn to step back when life becomes overwhelming. They're friends that guide you toward healthier relationships and choices. And hey, knowing when to walk away is important. Walking away from negativity is brave, not weak. It's a skill that takes practice but is worth it. I pray that you find the strength to let your "yes" and "no" reflect your values, just like Jesus showed. It's okay to step away from what harms you.

Boundaries are your friends, guiding you to a life of balance, love, and self-discovery.

**Scriptures:**

Proverbs 4:23:

*"Above all else, guard your heart, for everything you do flows from it."*

Philippians 4:7:

*"And the peace of God, which surpasses all understanding, will guard your hearts and minds through Christ Jesus."*

Galatians 5:22-23:

*"But the fruit of the Spirit is love, joy, peace, longsuffering, kindness, goodness, faithfulness, gentleness, self-control. Against such there is no law."*

1 Corinthians 6:19-20:

*"Or do you not know that your body is the temple of the Holy Spirit who is in you, whom you have from God, and you are not your own?  For you were bought at a price; therefore glorify God in your body and in your spirit, which are God's."*

Psalm 139:14:

*"I will praise You, for I am fearfully and wonderfully made; marvelous are Your works, and that my soul knows very well."*

1 Corinthians 10:23:

*"All things are lawful for me, but not all things are helpful; all things are lawful for me, but not all things edify."*

James 1:19:

*"So then, my beloved brethren, let every man be swift to hear, slow to speak, slow to wrath."*

Psalm 46:10:

*"Be still, and know that I am God; I will be exalted among the nations, I will be exalted in the earth."*

Ephesians 4:29:

*"Let no corrupt word proceed out of your mouth, but what is good for necessary edification, that it may impart grace to the hearers."*

Matthew 11:28–30:

*"Come to Me, all you who labor and are heavy laden, and I will give you rest. Take My yoke upon you and learn from Me, for I am gentle and lowly in heart, and you will find rest for your souls. For My yoke is easy, and My burden is light."*

**Prayer Points:**

1. Heavenly Father, as I embark on this journey to explore the concept of boundaries, I pray that You will open my

heart and mind to understand their significance. May I see boundaries as friendly guides, leading me towards a healthier and more purposeful life.

2. Dear Lord, if I have not yet recognized boundaries as companions on my journey, I ask for the wisdom to embrace them. Help me understand that they are here to support me, guiding me towards a life of fulfillment and balance.

3. God, I recognize that within the boundaries I set lies a power I haven't fully tapped into. Grant me the courage and insight to understand that I have control over my life's direction, choices, and the energy I invest. May I use this power wisely and purposefully.

4. Loving Father, in a world filled with hurt and isolation, I pray that You guide me towards self-love as You desire. Help me recognize the importance of safeguarding my mental well-being through the boundaries I establish.

5. Lord, grant me the gift of self-control. As I align my actions with my decisions through boundaries, may I find strength in mastering myself and my responses. Let my self-control reflect Your presence within me.

6. Heavenly Father, as I navigate relationships and interactions, may I remember the biblical truth in Ephesians 4:15. Help me speak truth with love, fostering growth and understanding in my interactions with others.

7. Dear Lord, guide me as I set boundaries in my life. Help me discern what to allow and what to limit, for the sake of my well-being and my relationships. May my boundaries be like a well-crafted armor, guarding against distractions.

8. Lord Jesus, just as You found rest when needed, I seek Your guidance in knowing when to step back and find

renewal. Grant me the wisdom to recognize when life becomes overwhelming and the strength to prioritize my well-being.

9. God, give me the courage to walk away from negativity and harmful situations. Help me remember that choosing to step away is an act of bravery, not weakness. May my decisions reflect the love and value You have for me.

10. Heavenly Father, I pray that You grant me the wisdom to let my "yes" and "no" reflect my values, just as Jesus showed us. Give me the courage to step away from what harms me and to embrace the boundaries that guide me towards a life of balance, love, and self-discovery.

Reflect

# 12

# Loving Yourself Requires Hard Work

Let's talk about loving yourself in a powerful way. It's about diving into every corner of your life that God designed for you. Then, it's about rolling up your sleeves and working to make those dreams real. Now, in this world, we're part of it, but we're not shaped by it. So, here's my challenge in this chapter: let's get down to business!

Listen up, you're not just a random creation. You've been made with awe-inspiring care. You're wired to learn, invest in yourself, and grow into your best version. But here's the catch: all of this takes effort. You've got to ask some tough questions. Who are you deep down? What talents do you hold? Where's your path leading? What impact will you make on your community? It's about your purpose on this earth.

Look around you, all those amazing things you see – they're fruits of hard work. God's kids can't ignore that side of life. We've got to put in the sweat. So, here's my encouragement for you: embrace the hustle. But here's a key part: learning to connect with the right people. It's about finding safe spaces to ask questions and get answers. Remember, we've talked about boundaries before, and they're like a safety net here. Speaking of which, accountability matters. The Bible says in 1 Thessalonians 5:11 that we should lift each other up. So, stand tall, no excuses.

Building strong relationships is a treasure. They reflect who you are. You've heard it, "Show me your friends, and I'll show who you are." Your ability to engage, connect, and build trust with others – that's a golden trait. And hey, as a child of God, it's vital to be trustworthy too. It's a two-way street.

Don't underestimate the power of dedication. Consistency is key in your journey to become your best self. Oh, and here's another piece: your whole self-matters. Your body, mind, and spirit are all interconnected. So, taking good care of these three parts is essential.

Speaking of trust, reliability is a jewel. Being consistent shows others your character. Remember, "Let your yes be yes, and your no be no." This helps you stand strong.

Becoming your best self is a challenge. Success, as God envisions it, takes serious hard work. Your story is like no other. Your identity is unique. Your DNA, and your background – they're all part of God's masterpiece. So, embrace every piece of yourself. Find strength in your uniqueness and put in the sweat to be the very best you.

Hold on, I'm not done yet. As you walk the path to your best self, remember this: Giving back is like a secret ingredient. When you share, you fill others' cups and yours. It's not just about taking; it's about generously giving, expecting nothing in return.

As you travel this journey, never forget to turn to prayer and God's word. Speak positivity over your life and write down your goals. And remember, God cares about every single detail of your life. From sunrise to moonlight, He's there. Trust Him in every step of your journey to become your best self, the version He has in mind. And don't let failures define you – they're steppingstones to growth. So, put in the hard work because nothing great comes easy. Calculate the effort, set values for all areas of your life, and most importantly, keep Jesus at the forefront of it all.

**Scriptures:**

Jeremiah 29:11:
*"For I know the thoughts that I think toward you, says the Lord, thoughts of peace and not of evil, to give you a future and a hope."*

Psalm 139:14:
*"I will praise You, for I am fearfully and wonderfully made; marvelous are Your works, and that my soul knows very well."*

Philippians 4:13:
*"I can do all things through Christ who strengthens me."*

Ephesians 2:10:
*"For we are His workmanship, created in Christ Jesus for good works, which God prepared beforehand that we should walk in them."*

Proverbs 27:17:

"As iron sharpens iron, so a man sharpens the countenance of his friend."

1 Corinthians 12:27:

"Now you are the body of Christ, and members individually."

Galatians 6:9:

"And let us not grow weary while doing good, for in due season we shall reap if we do not lose heart."

Matthew 5:16:

"Let your light so shine before men, that they may see your good works and glorify your Father in heaven."

1 Peter 5:7:

"Casting all your care upon Him, for He cares for you."

Proverbs 3:5-6:

"Trust in the Lord with all your heart, and lean not on your own understanding; in all your ways acknowledge Him, and He shall direct your paths."

**Prayer Points:**

1. Dear Lord, as I journey to embrace every corner of my life that You've designed for me, help me uncover the depths of who I am and discover my true purpose on this earth. Guide me to walk confidently in the path You've laid out

for me.

2. Heavenly Father, grant me the strength and determination to roll up my sleeves and work diligently towards making my dreams a reality. In the face of challenges, remind me of the value of hard work and perseverance.

3. Lord, help me cultivate relationships that reflect Your love and character. Teach me to engage, connect, and build trust with others, so that my interactions may be a testimony of Your grace.

4. Dear God, I ask for the discipline to stay consistent and reliable in all I do. Let my actions align with my words, and help me stand strong with integrity, just as You are faithful to us.

5. Heavenly Father, thank You for creating me as a unique masterpiece. Give me the courage to embrace every piece of myself, finding strength in my individuality as I strive to be the best version of me.

6. Lord, open my heart to the joy of giving back. May I generously share with others, knowing that through my actions, I am not only filling their cups but also receiving Your blessings in return.

7. Dear God, as I navigate this journey of self-improvement, be my guiding light. Help me speak positivity over my life, write down my goals, and remind me that You care for every detail.

8. Heavenly Father, in moments of uncertainty, remind me to trust in Your plan. Guide my steps as I strive to become the best version of myself, always keeping You at the forefront of my journey.

9. Lord, when failures come my way, let me not be discouraged. Instead, help me view them as stepping stones to

growth. Grant me the strength to rise above challenges, knowing that You are with me.

10. Dear Lord, I commit every area of my life to You. Help me set values aligned with Your Word and walk in faith, knowing that with Your grace, I can overcome obstacles and become the person You've destined me to be.

Reflect

# 13

## Embracing a Future Beyond Present Worries

Let's embark on a journey through the life of Joseph, a story many of us hold dear. Imagine being tossed into a world of adversity, sold by your own kin due to their jealousy. This very fate befell Joseph, carried away by a traveling merchant, and later, into the land of Egypt as a slave to Potiphar. Remarkably, his spirit remained unbroken, for he found prosperity even amid hardship, guided by the unwavering presence of God. The unfolding narrative reveals that Potiphar, perceptive to the blessing within Joseph, entrusted him with all he owned. But, alas, a new challenge emerged when Potiphar's wife falsely accused him, leading to his imprisonment. Potiphar's decision was swayed by a desire to vindicate his spouse, putting Joseph behind bars.

In this dark chapter, the story takes an unexpected turn. In prison, Joseph's unique gift surfaced as he interpreted dreams, even catching the attention of the Pharaoh. This instance unveils a profound truth: Joseph didn't credit his own abilities but rather attributed them to God's guiding hand.

The Pharaoh's trust in Joseph's interpretation led him to be appointed ruler over Egypt. What resonates deeply is Joseph's humility, as he declares, "I can't, but God helps me." The Pharaoh recognized the truth in his words, entrusting him with great authority. Joseph's journey, though condensed, speaks volumes of his resilience.

Joseph's journey isn't far from our own lives. Amidst trials, remember that challenges are fleeting. Just as Joseph confronted his brothers with courage, so can we confront our adversities with newfound strength. Let's take solace in knowing that today's worries will soon be a distant memory. Despite the strains of stress and anxiety, rest assured that these burdens will be cast aside. It's challenging to face present difficulties while gazing at a promising horizon. But even in the depths of emotions like depression, anxiety, and anger, remember, the adversities before us will soon be a thing of the past.

The tale continues with Joseph's family relocating to Egypt, invited by Pharaoh to oversee his livestock. Over time, Pharaohs grew wary of their increasing numbers, leading to heavier toil. It's a situation that mirrors our own struggles, where our efforts seem to lead to more hardship. But in these moments, take heart: what seems difficult today might yield abundant blessings tomorrow. While it might appear that the enemy holds sway, remember that our God can transform our circumstances for the better. When your hard work feels futile, keep the faith, for its rewards are on the horizon. When God urges you to "Go," it's time to take that leap. Despite the fear, remember that your inner potential is remarkable. Embrace the discomfort of growth, as it's through challenges that our talents truly shine.

**Scriptures:**

Romans 8:28:

*"And we know that all things work together for good to those who love God, to those who are the called according to His purpose."*

James 1:2-3:

*"My brethren, count it all joy when you fall into various trials, knowing that the testing of your faith produces patience."*

Isaiah 41:10:

*"Fear not, for I am with you; be not dismayed, for I am your God. I will strengthen you, yes, I will help you, I will uphold you with My righteous right hand."*

Psalm 27:1:

*"The Lord is my light and my salvation; whom shall I fear? The Lord is the strength of my life; of whom shall I be afraid?"*

2 Corinthians 4:17:

*"For our light affliction, which is but for a moment, is working for us a far more exceeding and eternal weight of glory."*

Philippians 4:6-7:

*"Be anxious for nothing, but in everything by prayer and supplication, with thanksgiving, let your requests be made known to God; and the peace of God, which*

*surpasses all understanding, will guard your hearts and minds through Christ Jesus."*

Matthew 11:28-30:

*"Come to Me, all you who labor and are heavy laden, and I will give you rest. Take My yoke upon you and learn from Me, for I am gentle and lowly in heart, and you will find rest for your souls."*

Jeremiah 29:11:

*"For I know the thoughts that I think toward you, says the Lord, thoughts of peace and not of evil, to give you a future and a hope."*

1 Peter 5:7:

*"Casting all your care upon Him, for He cares for you."*

Proverbs 16:3:

*"Commit your works to the Lord, and your thoughts will be established."*

**Prayer Points:**

1. Dear Heavenly Father, like Joseph, I may face adversity and challenges in my life. Please grant me the strength to remain unbroken, guided by Your unwavering presence. Help me find prosperity even in the midst of hardships, knowing that Your plans for me are good. Amen.
2. Loving God, just as Joseph attributed his unique gifts to

Your guiding hand, help me recognize that my abilities are from You. Grant me the humility to acknowledge that I can't do it alone, but with Your help, I can achieve great things. Amen.

3. Dear Lord, give me the courage to confront my adversities with newfound strength, just as Joseph confronted his brothers. Help me take solace in the fact that today's worries will soon fade, and the burdens I carry will be cast aside. Amen.

4. Heavenly Father, in moments of stress, anxiety, and anger, grant me peace. Remind me that the adversities I face will soon be a thing of the past, and that Your love and grace are ever-present. Amen.

5. Gracious God, when my efforts seem to lead to more hardships, help me remember that divine laws can transform my circumstances for the better. Keep me steadfast in faith, knowing that the rewards of my hard work are on the horizon. Amen.

6. Dear Lord, help me embrace my vision just as Joseph's family embraced the opportunity in Egypt. Strengthen my resolve to push beyond obstacles and fulfill the purpose You have for my life. May my actions reflect my clear mission. Amen.

7. Heavenly Father, like the courageous mother who protected her child, guide me to overcome my past fears and traumas. Reveal the untapped potential within me, whether it's a God-given gift or a latent aspiration. Help me emerge and shine for Your glory. Amen.

8. Loving God, when You whisper "Go," give me the courage to take that leap of faith. Despite my fears and doubts, remind me that whatever is within me is extraordinary.

Help me embrace the discomfort of growth, knowing it leads to true fulfillment. Amen.

9. Dear Lord, when my efforts seem futile and hardship weighs me down, grant me the faith to trust Your plans for my life. Help me understand that challenges today may lead to abundant blessings tomorrow. Amen.

10. Gracious Heavenly Father, I thank You for the inspirational journey of Joseph. May his story be a source of encouragement for me and all who face trials. Give us the strength to persevere, the wisdom to embrace growth, and the faith to trust in Your divine guidance. Amen.

Reflect

14

# Birthing Alignment With Wisdom, Strategy, And Prayer

Let's delve into the inspiring tale of Jochebed, the mother of Moses. In a time of great turmoil, she gave birth to her son when an order to eliminate all male children was in effect. Initially, she managed to conceal her baby's existence, but the inevitable moment arrived when hiding was no longer an option. This narrative holds a profound message: When the time is ripe, there's no delaying the birthing of ideas, creativity, and aspirations. The call to bring forth something remarkable cannot be ignored. If you sense the moment is now, heed that call and release what's within you.

In the pages of scripture, we witness Jochebed's strategic move. When she could no longer hide her son, she crafted a basket, placing him afloat on the river Nile. She stepped further by positioning her daughter at a vantage point to observe his journey. Strategy played a vital role. Consider strategic planning as you prepare to give birth to your well-formed concepts, just as did. Strategize like Jochebed did—putting mechanisms in place to witness the unfolding.

Yet, remember this: birthing your gift can be uncomfortable. You must be willing to emerge and triumph over limitations, discomfort, and stagnation. As the story unfolds, we see how Pharaoh's daughter discovered the baby in the basket. She recognized his beauty and his heritage. Rather than reporting it, she was moved with compassion. In this, we glimpse a truth: God sometimes orchestrates circumstances to confound your adversaries, turning their efforts in your favor. As you approach your birthing season, invoke prayer to release the angels assigned to guide you, to forge ahead on your behalf.

We know the enemy seeks to still, kill and destroy. Yet, sometimes, you must engage in a form of spiritual warfare. By rallying your faith, by kneeling in fervent prayer, you call upon the angelic forces of the Lord to precede your path. This is your declaration of war against the forces of opposition.

Continuing in the narrative, Jochebed's daughter seized a strategic opportunity. She offered to find a nursemaid for the child, and this is where your network comes into play. Surround yourself with allies who align with your purpose and amplify your strengths. Forge connections that complement your journey.

I often refer to these individuals as "purpose partners." They are the ones sent by the Lord during your specific season to assist you in the process of "birthing" your purpose, and to guide you through what lies ahead. Just as Proverbs 27:17 reminds us, *"As iron sharpens iron, so one person sharpens another."* These purpose partners are here to help you fulfill your God-given destiny, sharpen your skills, and provide vital support in your current season. Whether you are giving birth to a new idea, navigating challenges at work, or contributing to your community, these individuals are the ones God has placed in your life to strengthen and sharpen you.

Just as God brings people into your life to assist, remember that the enemy also seeks to sow discord. Therefore, it's vital to discern and identify your purpose partners for your season of birthing. I encourage you to pray for guidance and wisdom, asking God to help you recognize these individuals so that you can birth your purpose with divine assistance.

As you navigate this chapter of birthing, push through any barriers. Network with purposeful intent and infuse every step with prayer. By aligning your efforts with the will of God, you secure a birthing that is not only successful but also peaceful.

Embrace this path with determination, lean into the wisdom of strategy, and let prayer be your guide. May your birthing be a testament to your alignment with divine purpose.

**Scriptures:**

Ecclesiastes 3:1:
*"To everything there is a season, a time for every purpose under heaven."*

Proverbs 16:9:
*"A man's heart plans his way, but the Lord directs his steps."*

Isaiah 55:11:
*"So shall My word be that goes forth from My mouth; it shall not return to Me void, but it shall accomplish what I please, and it shall prosper in the thing for which I sent it."*

Jeremiah 29:11:

*"For I know the thoughts that I think toward you, says the Lord, thoughts of peace and not of evil, to give you a future and a hope."*

Psalm 27:1:

*"The Lord is my light and my salvation; whom shall I fear? The Lord is the strength of my life; of whom shall I be afraid?"*

Philippians 4:13:

*"I can do all things through Christ who strengthens me."*

Romans 8:28:

*"And we know that all things work together for good to those who love God, to those who are the called according to His purpose."*

Isaiah 41:10:

*"Fear not, for I am with you; be not dismayed, for I am your God. I will strengthen you, yes, I will help you, I will uphold you with My righteous right hand."*

2 Corinthians 10:4:

*"For the weapons of our warfare are not carnal but mighty in God for pulling down strongholds."*

Psalm 139:16:

*"Your eyes saw my substance, being yet unformed. And*

*in Your book they all were written, the days fashioned for me, when as yet there were none of them."*

**Prayer Points:**

1. Heavenly Father, just as Jochebed obeyed the call to bring forth something remarkable, I seek Your guidance in discerning the perfect timing for birthing my ideas and aspirations. Help me recognize the signs of readiness and give me the courage to release what's within me when the moment is ripe. Amen.

2. Dear Lord, as I embark on this journey of birthing creativity and purpose, grant me the wisdom to strategize like Jochebed and Joshua. May I craft thoughtful plans and set mechanisms in motion to witness the unfolding of my well-formed concepts. Guide my steps as I prepare to share my gifts with the world. Amen.

3. Loving God, I understand that birthing my gift may come with discomfort and challenges. Just as Jochebed faced the inevitable moment of revealing her son, give me the strength to emerge from limitations, overcome stagnation, and triumph over adversity. I trust that the rewards of this journey are worth the discomfort. Amen.

4. Merciful Lord, like Pharaoh's daughter who was moved with compassion, I believe that You can orchestrate circumstances to confound my adversaries. As I approach my birthing season, I invoke Your presence and the guidance of angels to lead me on the path You've set before me. May my challenges be turned into opportunities by Your divine

hand. Amen.

5. Mighty God, I recognize that the enemy seeks to obstruct and undermine my efforts. Today, I declare my faith as a weapon against opposition. By kneeling in fervent prayer, I call upon Your angelic forces to precede my path, thwarting the schemes of the enemy. I engage in spiritual warfare with confidence in Your victory. Amen.

6. Dear Lord, just as Jochebed's daughter played a strategic role in the narrative, I understand the importance of networking with purpose. Surround me with allies who share my purpose and amplify my strengths. May my connections complement my journey and contribute to the success of my birthing process. Amen.

7. Heavenly Father, guide me as I navigate this chapter of birthing. Help me push through barriers and challenges, all while aligning my efforts with Your divine will. May my journey be marked by Your peace, and may my actions be a testament to my alignment with Your purpose for my life. Amen.

8. Loving God, grant me determination as I tread the path of birthing my creative gifts. Just as Jochebed's actions were marked by determination, I lean into the wisdom of strategy and planning. May my steps be guided by Your wisdom, and may my efforts bear fruit that glorifies Your name. Amen.

9. Gracious Lord, in this journey of birthing, I seek Your guidance and insight. Help me see beyond the surface, just as Jochebed saw the potential in the river Nile. Open my eyes to opportunities that align with Your purpose for me. May my every step be marked by divine revelation. Amen.

10. Dear God, as I embrace the path of birthing, I invite Your blessings upon this journey. May my efforts be fruitful, and may the gifts I bring forth inspire and uplift others. Bless my endeavors with success, and may my birthing be a testament to Your grace, guidance, and divine purpose. Amen.

Reflect

# 15

# Stepping Into a Season of Glory and New Dimensions

et us transition from a state of solace to a state of magnificence, for God is ready to receive all the glory as we push forward and unleash all He has entrusted to us. This journey is one of profound transformation and demands unwavering faith and a belief that God's hand is actively at work within us.  In His humble way, He will bring forth His glory in our lives, much like Joseph's emergence from the depths of a pit to become a ruler or David's transformation from a simple shepherd boy to a mighty king.  Your significance is unquestionable, and God yearns to manifest His new wonders in your life. So, let us boldly transition from comfort to glory, for such is His divine intent.

However, this transition relies not solely on our strength but on His abundant grace. By His grace, we will navigate this shift, and by His grace, we will step into the splendor of His glory. He will guide us from obscurity to prominence, holding us through our journey.  The adversities and challenges we face today will soon fade into the background. Therefore, persist in your efforts, for this journey is not solely about you. It is intricately tied to the purpose of His Kingdom and the generations that will follow. Emerge from the shadows with determination, as tribulations draw you nearer to God. Know that He will pave a path where none seems to exist. Reflect upon the fact that your current circumstances would drastically differ without God's intervention. His unchanging nature remains steadfast—yesterday, today, and forever. His concern is not merely for ideal circumstances; He cares about your situation. So, do not let your current setbacks or letdowns cloud your vision or deter you from your mission. Instead, entrust your vision and mission entirely to Him.

The Lord has been your companion since the beginning, and His presence will not waver from this day onward. The transition journey may not be seamless but do not hesitate to offer your gifts to God. Break through the obstacles that lie ahead and emerge victoriously. Remember the words of Joseph: "I am Joseph, I am not dead." In the same way, recognize that you are not defeated. As long as breath fills your lungs and life courses through your veins, you can read these words, walk, talk, perceive the world around you, and much more. God's purpose for you remains unfulfilled. He is both the originator and the completer of your faith.

I encourage you to step forward and claim your rightful place as a child of God. Declare that this is your season to transition from obscurity to glory. Affirm that the anointing which shatters every bond is upon you. Proclaim that you are entering a realm of new dimensions. Declare that success will flourish in all facets of your life—your ministry, children, ideas, creativity, and ventures. Remember, this transformation is not fueled by your strength alone but by the blazing fire of the

Almighty. And as you stand firm, remember that He is Jehovah-Gabor, the invincible and mighty God. Just as He does not falter, you will not falter. Be uplifted by these words and may God's blessings be abundant upon you.

**Scriptures:**

Isaiah 43:19:

*"Behold, I will do a new thing, now it shall spring forth; shall you not know it?  I will even make a road in the wilderness and rivers in the desert."*

Romans 12:2:

*"And do not be conformed to this world, but be transformed by the renewing of your mind, that you may prove what is that good and acceptable and perfect will of God."*

2 Corinthians 3:18:

*"But we all, with unveiled face, beholding as in a mirror the glory of the Lord, are being transformed into the same image from glory to glory, just as by the Spirit of the Lord."*

Philippians 4:13:

*"I can do all things through Christ who strengthens me."*

Psalm 37:23:

*"The steps of a good man are ordered by the Lord, and He delights in his way."*

Jeremiah 29:11:

*"For I know the thoughts that I think toward you, says the Lord, thoughts of peace and not of evil, to give you a future and a hope."*

Hebrews 13:8:

*"Jesus Christ is the same yesterday, today, and forever."*

Psalm 138:8:

*"The Lord will perfect that which concerns me; Your mercy, O Lord, endures forever; do not forsake the works of Your hands."*

Isaiah 41:10:

*"Fear not, for I am with you; be not dismayed, for I am your God. I will strengthen you, yes, I will help you, I will uphold you with My righteous right hand."*

Ephesians 2:10:

*"For we are His workmanship, created in Christ Jesus for good works, which God prepared beforehand that we should walk in them."*

**Prayer Points:**

1. Heavenly Father, as I embark on this journey of transformation, I pray for the strength to transition from solace to magnificence. May Your glory shine through as I unleash the gifts You've entrusted to me. Guide me

with unwavering faith. Amen.

2. Lord, in Your humble way, bring forth Your glory in my life, just as You did for Joseph and David. I embrace the significance You've placed within me and eagerly transition from comfort to Your divine intent. Amen.

3. Gracious God, I acknowledge that this transition is not about my strength, but Your abundant grace. Lead me from obscurity to prominence, and guide me through challenges. I persist in faith, knowing Your purpose spans generations. Amen.

4. Father, I emerge from shadows with determination, drawing closer to You through tribulations. Your path will be revealed, and I trust Your intervention in my circumstances. May my setbacks not deter me from Your mission for my life. Amen.

5. Lord, I declare that Your presence is unwavering as I journey through transition. With Your help, I overcome obstacles and offer my gifts to You. I hold onto Your promise that I am not defeated but transformed. Amen.

6. Heavenly Father, I step into my season of transition with confidence. I affirm that Your anointing breaks every bond. I embrace new dimensions and declare success in every facet of my life. This transformation is powered by Your fire. Amen.

7. Lord, as I stand firm in Your invincible might, I claim Your blessings upon this journey. Just as You have been with me since the beginning, I trust Your guiding hand. May my life be a testament to Your glory. Amen.

8. God, I entrust my vision and mission entirely to You. Guide me through this journey, knowing that You are the originator and completer of my faith. I claim my place as

Your child and declare this transition is marked by Your divine purpose. Amen.

9. Loving Father, I proclaim my entry into new dimensions, as I step out of obscurity into Your glorious plan. May the fire of Your presence fuel my transformation, and may my life radiate the invincibility of Jehovah-Gabor. Amen.

10. Heavenly Father, I am uplifted by Your words of promise. As I transition from comfort to glory, I embrace Your blessings. Let Your abundant grace guide me, and may Your magnificent plan unfold in every area of my life. Amen.

Reflect

# 16

# Embracing the Wilderness: Perseverance in Spiritual Dryness

I remember getting up in the middle of the night, going into the bathroom, and just crying my heart out. I felt lonely. I felt like I was not where I was supposed to be. I felt dark. I felt like I didn't have control. I felt like everything around me just seemed to be... quiet, dark, even though I was in the midst of one of the joyful times of my life. This was me in my wilderness, dealing with postpartum depression.

My third pregnancy was extremely difficult, so I started to emotionally withdraw. Physically, I wasn't able to keep up with my day-to-day. I could no longer work. I could no longer do a lot of things that I am used to, or a lot of things that keep me busy. That was a very dark, dark time, even though in the middle of the light, it was a very challenging time for me. I felt like I was losing my mind. I felt like tomorrow was too far. I couldn't recognize myself. Combing my hair was difficult. Brushing my teeth was difficult. Dressing up was difficult.

During this time, man, I could not pray. I could only rely on my husband's prayers. I could only rely on the people who probably thought of me and prayed for me. I could only rely on my previous prayers, my prayer bank. And I'll call this time spiritual wilderness, spiritual dryness. I thank God for my prayer bank, but I felt dry. Because the word of God says that our cup needs to run over. So for me, even feeling halfway full or halfway empty felt like me being dry.

The season where I could not pour into other people's lives was a season where I couldn't even recognize what was inside my cup. Was I half full? Was I half empty? I wasn't able to make that assessment. I felt like mentally... I believe if you're spiritually dry, everything else is... Everything else is more... you sense other things more. So emotionally, I felt it more. Psychologically, I felt it more.

And it was very funny because again, I had my baby, so that was one of the best. I was so happy when I saw her, so happy knowing that she's safe, she's alive. But yet that moment was still there. So sometimes things are going right around you, but you yourself, you are in a space where you are in a dry place spiritually. And that also can be a very difficult place to be. It doesn't show that. It shows that God is far. You feel like you've failed at something.

It was so powerful that, you know, some of the few seconds that I could get to think emotionally and to think usually, like the places where I was where I could think effectively, the small moment that I gained in the midst of this dryness. Like I say, when I talk about dryness, I'm not talking about completely dry, where I don't know who Jesus is, right? It's my spiritual dryness I tried to know that my cup was, you know, halfway full or halfway dry.

You know, you're in a state of a lot of confusion, but there's some moments there because the Bible said truly, He never leaves nor forsakes us. So we might be in a space where we feel that we do not hear Jesus or we do not hear the Lord or the Lord is far away, but that's never true. It is our own reality of what is happening and how we're interpreting it.

But it's so powerful when you're able to identify those or when you're able to find yourself in those small moments where you can think critically and be like, okay, this is just a stressful time. This is a time where, yes, my mind, my body maybe are telling me something, but it's not my truth, right?

It's maybe the reality of what I'm facing now. Yes, I'm feeling those emotions, which is completely true because those are true feelings. They're not fake feelings. You're feeling sad. You're feeling down. You're feeling like everything is dark, and those are true feelings. Those are real feelings, but they're not the truth.

The truth is Jesus never leaves a nor forsakes us. The truth is that our God is always a second away. The truth is our God never leaves us. The truth is we have more than we can account for at that time. So those small moments when I could identify, I could think, I look at my child and say, Lord, thank you. Thank you that we made it out of the hospital regardless of what the doctor said, that I was not going to make it. Thank you that my daughter is here today even though her sugar was at 14. For those that are in the medical field, it was a ridiculous number. She was not supposed to be here, but thank you that she's here.

The small moment that you get in your dryness, use that and give God small praise. It's okay. Use those moments to cry out to God. It might be a few seconds. It might be a few minutes. It's okay to be in that space whenever you are able to.

So be able to really target those small moments that you are recognizing the small strength that you have. Because when we are weak, we are strong. So there are moments in this wilderness or this dryness that you have moments of acknowledging that Christ is still here, that I'm still alive, that I'm still breathing. You still have that chance. So understanding the spiritual dryness and what comes with it.

I want to encourage you to continue to persevere in the middle of your dryness. The role of perseverance in spiritual growth is key. This journey that we are in, this thing called life, is what it's all about. We do have ups and downs and dryness. You have times where your cup's close until the run is over, where you're able to pour into other people's lives. And you have times where you need people to pour into your lives. You have times where your cup is either half full or half dry. That is life. But one thing is for sure that even though we endure for a time, light comes in the morning. It is for a season, and that season will pass. Tomorrow always comes.

So I want to encourage you that in a space where you're feeling dry, remember to persevere. Persevere when you face adversities. Persevere when you feel lonely. Persevere when you feel confused. Persevere when you feel tired. Persevere knowing that tomorrow always comes. And one thing that kept me during this time is the fact that I had to persevere for my family. I had to persevere for my children. I had to persevere for the kingdom. Life was more than just me.

I think once you have this into perspective, you get to appreciate what you are, and you get the strength to persevere, and the strength to keep moving forward. And also, the more you go through those times, the more spiritually mature you become. The more you go through those challenges, you find yourself becoming stronger and stronger. You find yourself, if you had to go through a similar situation, you'll be a little bit better because you can remember. Because God has given you that gift to be able to remember. The gift to remember where He took you from. The gift to remember where you were yesterday. The gift to remember where God took you from, from the Mary cliff.

We all have a story somewhere. We all have something that we can say, 'I remember.' It could be in your childhood. It could be now. It could be at work. It could be a situation that happened. But you know if it wasn't for God on your side, you wouldn't have made it. So sometimes it's also good to dig deep into those places and remember. The gift of remembrance. It brings you to a place of spiritual maturity.

So I want to encourage you. During this time, not to give up. Not to give up. As Christians, we need to embrace the wilderness. It's not easy. We don't call for it. It just comes. We don't know the hours. Sometimes we don't know the time. It just comes. But when it comes, thank God for Jesus. When it comes, thank God that we have someone that is greater than us. When it comes, thank God that we have the one who created heaven and earth. The one who knows you before you were born in your mother's womb. That person is with us at all times. He's always on our side. So overcome the doubt and overcome the fears when you're by yourself in that wilderness.

And one thing is for sure is that we need to remain patient. When I found myself in that place, I needed it to go away right away. I wanted it to go away in a second. But I believe that God teaches us patience in those situations. Hallelujah. So always remember that your dry season is never a surprise to God. It is just part of this journey called life. Remember that stress, doubt, and all of those things are caused by the trigger are the triggers due to your dryness. And also remember that this too shall pass. There's light at the end of the tunnel and tomorrow always comes. Even the one that is with you, Jesus, even death cannot hold them captive. And that's the kind of God that you serve. That's the kind of God that we go up to. So embrace your dry season when it comes. Tap into those small moments where you can thank the Lord and acknowledge His presence there with you. And know that it's not over until God says it's over. And you're always on the winning side.

**Scriptures:**

Psalm 34:17-18:
*"The righteous cry out, and the Lord hears, and delivers them out of all their troubles. The Lord is near to those who have a broken heart, and saves such as have a contrite spirit."*

Isaiah 41:10:
*"Fear not, for I am with you; be not dismayed, for I am your God. I will strengthen you, yes, I will help you, I will uphold you with My righteous right hand."*

2 Corinthians 12:9:
*"And He said to me, 'My grace is sufficient for you, for My strength is made perfect in weakness.' Therefore most gladly I will rather boast in my infirmities, that the power of Christ may rest upon me."*

Psalm 42:11:
*"Why are you cast down, O my soul? And why are you disquieted within me? Hope in God; for I shall yet praise*

*Him, the help of my countenance and my God."*

Romans 8:38-39:

*"For I am persuaded that neither death nor life, nor angels nor principalities nor powers, nor things present nor things to come, nor height nor depth, nor any other created thing, shall be able to separate us from the love of God which is in Christ Jesus our Lord."*

Psalm 23:4:

*"Yea, though I walk through the valley of the shadow of death, I will fear no evil; for You are with me; Your rod and Your staff, they comfort me."*

Philippians 4:13:

*"I can do all things through Christ who strengthens me."*

Psalm 30:5:

*"For His anger is but for a moment, His favor is for life; weeping may endure for a night, but joy comes in the morning."*

James 1:2-4:

*"My brethren, count it all joy when you fall into various trials, knowing that the testing of your faith produces patience. But let patience have its perfect work, that you may be perfect and complete, lacking nothing."*

Hebrews 13:5:

*"Let your conduct be without covetousness; be content with such things as you have. For He Himself has said, 'I will never leave you nor forsake you.'"*

## Prayer Points:

1. Dear Lord, in the midst of my darkness and loneliness, I cry out to You. Please comfort my heart and bring relief to my soul. Help me find the light in the midst of this challenging season.

2. Heavenly Father, grant me the strength to regain control over my emotions and my life. Help me overcome the feeling of losing myself and guide me towards a path of healing.

3. Lord, restore my emotional well-being. Lift the heaviness from my heart and mind. Let your joy replace my sadness, and help me to see the beauty in life once again.

4. Dear God, even in my spiritual dryness, I know You are near. Please reveal Your presence to me and help me feel Your closeness, especially when I feel distant.

5. Father, I thank You for the small moments of clarity and strength amidst my struggles. Help me to recognize and cherish these moments as gifts from You.

6. Lord, I trust in Your promise that You will never forsake me. Even in my doubts and confusion, help me hold onto the truth of Your unwavering presence in my life.

7. Heavenly Father, grant me the perseverance to endure this spiritual wilderness. Help me to keep moving forward, knowing that this season too shall pass.

8. God, use this time of trial to mold me into a spiritually mature person. May I emerge from this darkness stronger, with a deeper understanding of Your love and grace.

9. Lord, teach me patience during this challenging time. Help me to trust Your timing and to wait upon You, knowing that You are working in my life.

10. Lord, I surrender my fears and doubts to You. I choose to embrace this wilderness, knowing that You are with me and that I am always on the winning side with You by my side.

## Reflect

# 17

# My Tiny Seed

That day I remember my stomach feeling like I was going to throw up. I was shaking, I was anxious, I even started sweating. I was so distressed. If you really ask me why, I'm not sure that I have a specific answer as to why I felt the way I felt. But before coming out with my foundation, OULA Foundation, I had so much anxiety. That today I sit back and I wonder why. And it really, really was a time when the enemy, that time showed me how much the enemy is wicked. And how much it's so important to make sure that the only voice that you hear and pound your arm is that of the Lord.

I remember feelings like, *"Who do you think you are? You are such a young girl, you don't have a lot of wisdom. You don't have enough money. What kind of change can you make in the world? Why do you think you're special?"* I had the enemy tormenting my mind, trying to prevent me from starting my foundation. But it's amazing how I had to take a step of faith to push the button, to submit the application. I am so glad that I'm able to talk about this today. And all I can say is thank God.

It took faith for me to start the foundation. It took a very small amount of faith because I can tell you, I had fear all over me, I had anxiety all over me, but there was a small amount of faith somewhere in my heart that I was willing to plant. So I want to encourage you, just like the parable of the mustard seed in Matthew 13:31-32, allow your seed to grow. It cannot grow if you don't plant it. So don't think that it requires you to go to the gym and work out to build muscles before you plant a mustard seed. It's not true. The fact that you are living, breathing, that is all the strength you need to plant a small seed of faith with what God has called you to do, with the step that you need to take to enter your new season.

With all that was going on around me, with all that I was feeling, the anxiety, the fear, I found a small seed that I was able to plant and nurture. And as the scripture continues to say that that small seed of faith grew to a point where it then became a tree, where the birds could also benefit. So think about it. As you're planting this seed, you're not only going to see the fruit, but it's also going to be a blessing to other people. Today, my foundation has been a blessing to many people. We're able to minister to young girls. We're able to provide food to the less fortunate. We're able to give wheelchairs away to handicaps who could not walk. Look at God, what he did with a tiny, small faith. Look at what God was able to do with the fact that I was willing to plant a very tiny seed, regardless of how I was feeling or the anxiety or the negativity around me.

So I would like to encourage you. Faith starts small, and it's okay. Remember, what is most important is the right ground. And if God has called you to do something, he will provide for the vision that he has given you. Remember that a small faith that you plant, a small seed that you plant can grow and also be a blessing to other people.

**Scriptures:**

Matthew 17:20:

*"So Jesus said to them, 'Because of your unbelief; for assuredly, I say to you, if you have faith as a mustard seed, you will say to this mountain, 'Move from here to there,' and it will move; and nothing will be impossible for you.'"*

Philippians 4:6-7:

*"Be anxious for nothing, but in everything by prayer and supplication, with thanksgiving, let your requests be made known to God; and the peace of God, which surpasses all understanding, will guard your hearts and minds through Christ Jesus."*

Isaiah 41:10:

*"Fear not, for I am with you; be not dismayed, for I am your God. I will strengthen you, yes, I will help you, I will uphold you with My righteous right hand."*

Romans 8:31:

*"What then shall we say to these things? If God is for us, who can be against us?"*

2 Timothy 1:7:

*"For God has not given us a spirit of fear, but of power and of love and of a sound mind."*

Isaiah 43:1:

*"But now, thus says the Lord, who created you, O Jacob, and He who formed you, O Israel: 'Fear not, for I have redeemed you; I have called you by your name; You are Mine.'"*

Psalm 37:5:

*"Commit your way to the Lord, trust also in Him, and He shall bring it to pass."*

Jeremiah 29:11:

*"'For I know the thoughts that I think toward you,' says the Lord, 'thoughts of peace and not of evil, to give you a future and a hope.'"*

Proverbs 3:5-6:

*"Trust in the Lord with all your heart, and lean not on your own understanding; in all your ways acknowledge Him, and He shall direct your paths."*

Galatians 6:9:

*"And let us not grow weary while doing good, for in due season we shall reap if we do not lose heart."*

**Prayer Points:**

1. Dear Heavenly Father, in moments of fear and self-doubt, I pray for the courage to take that step of faith, just as the mustard seed grows into a mighty tree. Help me trust that I have all the strength I need to fulfill the purpose You've

placed in my heart.

2. Lord, when anxiety and distress grip my heart, remind me that You are my refuge and strength. May Your peace replace my fears, knowing that You are with me every step of the way.

3. Heavenly Father, in times when the enemy's voice is loud and discouraging, let me hear Your voice louder, guiding and reassuring me that I am chosen and special in Your eyes.

4. Lord Jesus, I pray for the strength to overcome the obstacles and doubts that try to prevent me from pursuing Your calling for my life. Help me push the button, submit the application, and step out in faith.

5. Gracious God, I thank You for the small seed of faith within my heart, even when surrounded by fear and negativity. Water that seed, Lord, and let it grow into something beautiful and fruitful for Your glory.

6. Father, grant me the wisdom and discernment to recognize the right ground for planting my faith. Help me find the fertile soil where Your purpose for my life can flourish.

7. Lord, I lift up my foundation and its mission to You. Bless it abundantly so that it may be a source of blessing to others, just as You have blessed me.

8. Heavenly Father, in moments of weakness, remind me that it's not the size of my faith that matters but the greatness of the God in whom I place my trust.

9. Lord, grant me the patience to nurture my faith as it grows, just as a tiny seed becomes a flourishing tree. Help me to see the fruit and blessings it brings not only to me but also to those around me.

10. Gracious God, I am thankful for the journey of faith and for

the assurance that You will provide for the vision You've given me. May my small faith lead to significant impact in Your name. Amen.

## Reflect

<h1 style="text-align:center">18</h1>

# The Power of Prayer and Discernment

What sets us apart as believers in the Lord is our profound ability to connect with Him and our unwavering desire to understand His will and follow it wholeheartedly. As children of God, our daily pursuit revolves around seeking His guidance and discerning His purpose for our lives on this earthly journey. Every day, we strive to align our actions with His will, recognizing that our life's purpose is to accomplish all that He has ordained for us in this world. The paramount importance of seeking God's guidance and the role of discernment cannot be overstated in the life of a believer. This chapter explores how prayer, the vital link that connects us with God, not only reveals His actions but also illuminates His ways, making discernment an achievable and transformative part of our journey.

Prayer serves as a profound means of communication with God. Often, we associate prayer with formal rituals, envisioning a posture of kneeling, scripted verses, or structured gatherings. However, there exists a compelling facet of prayer—a form I engage in daily. It's an inner dialogue, a communion of the soul, an unspoken connection with our Lord Jesus Christ.

In these personal moments with the God I express gratitude—simple words like 'thank you' and 'hallelujah' spring forth. I lay before Him my concerns, seeking His guidance and wisdom. I share my innermost thoughts, emotions, and dilemmas, as if He were my closest confidant. It's a continuous exchange, a genuine conversation between my heart and His.

I extend an earnest invitation to you: embrace this intimate avenue of prayer. It's a personal journey, unburdened by formality or rigidity. It keeps me grounded, serving as a constant reminder of God's presence in my life. While I advocate for one-on-one prayer with God, I also recognize the immense strength in communal prayer—uniting with fellow believers in powerful intercession. Yet, amidst the collective voices, I firmly believe that your individual dialogue with Jesus holds a distinct significance. Learn to converse with God in your unique way, just as you are, and let it be an authentic expression of your faith journey.

Indeed, prayer stands as the key to unlocking the mysteries of God's will in our lives. It is in the sanctified moments of prayer that we cultivate an intimacy with Jesus, learning His ways, discerning His purposes, and forging a connection that transcends the physical realm."

"In the tapestry of your daily existence, weave the thread of prayer seamlessly. Prayer should not be an isolated event but a continuous conversation with the Almighty. The essence lies not in imitation but in authenticity. Find what works best for you. It may begin with just a minute, a whispered utterance in your quietest moments. The key is to start where you are, with the time you have, for no one can pray on your behalf to build your relationship with Christ.

The journey of faith necessitates your active participation in the sacred act of prayer. It cannot be outsourced, transferred, or borrowed. While others can pray for your transformation and growth, the ultimate goal is for you to stand firmly, forging a personal relationship with Christ, and discerning His purpose for your life.

In the labyrinth of life's uncertainties, when anxiety grips your heart, or when decisions weigh heavily on your shoulders, recognize these as moments beckoning you to the altar of prayer. I vividly recall a season in my life when I yearned for a job change. The unease was palpable; I was overwhelmed by restlessness and anxiety. Despite my efforts and qualifications, new job opportunities remained elusive. It was as if the entire wold conspired against my plans.

In those trying moments, I realized the need to recalibrate. I turned to prayer, not as a last resort, but as a means to align myself with God's will. As I ventured into prayer anew, I found not just answers, but a profound sense of peace.

**Scriptures:**

Psalm 55:17:
*"Evening and morning and at noon I will pray, and cry aloud, and He shall hear my voice."*

Jeremiah 29:12:
*"Then you will call upon Me and go and pray to Me, and I will listen to you."*

Philippians 4:6-7:

*"Be anxious for nothing, but in everything by prayer and supplication, with thanksgiving, let your requests be made known to God; and the peace of God, which surpasses all understanding, will guard your hearts and minds through Christ Jesus."*

Matthew 6:6:

*"But you, when you pray, go into your room, and when you have shut your door, pray to your Father who is in the secret place; and your Father who sees in secret will reward you openly."*

James 5:16:

*"Confess your trespasses to one another, and pray for one another, that you may be healed.  The effective, fervent prayer of a righteous man avails much."*

Psalm 143:8:

*"Cause me to hear Your lovingkindness in the morning, for in You do I trust; cause me to know the way in which I should walk, for I lift up my soul to You."*

Matthew 18:20:

*"For where two or three are gathered together in My name, I am there in the midst of them."*

Romans 12:12:

*"Rejoicing in hope, patient in tribulation, continuing steadfastly in prayer."*

Isaiah 26:3:

*"You will keep him in perfect peace, whose mind is stayed on You, because he trusts in You."*

Psalm 34:17:

*"The righteous cry out, and the Lord hears, and delivers them out of all their troubles."*

**Prayer Points:**

1. Dear Lord, I come before you with a heart full of gratitude. Thank you for the profound ability to connect with you, for the unwavering desire to understand your will, and for the privilege of following it wholeheartedly. I am thankful for the daily pursuit of seeking your guidance and discerning your purpose in my life.

2. Heavenly Father, guide my steps each day so that I may align my actions with your perfect will. Help me recognize that my life's purpose is to accomplish all that you have ordained for me in this world.

3. Lord, grant me the gift of discernment. Let me see your ways and understand your purpose clearly as I navigate this earthly journey. May I always distinguish your voice from the noise of the world.

4. Dear God, help me embrace the intimate avenue of prayer in its truest form. Let my prayers be a genuine conversation between my heart and yours, unburdened by formality or rigidity. Teach me to come before you just as I am.

5. Lord, I acknowledge the strength in communal prayer. May our collective voices rise to you in powerful inter-

cession. In our unity, help us draw closer to you and to each other.

6. Heavenly Father, in the sanctified moments of prayer, grant me the peace that surpasses understanding. Help me to cultivate intimacy with you and learn your ways. Let me feel your presence, knowing that it transcends the physical realm.

7. Lord, I pray that prayer becomes a continuous conversation with you, not just an isolated event. In my quietest moments, let me whisper my thoughts and desires to you. May my relationship with you grow stronger each day.

8. Dear God, I understand that my faith journey necessitates my active participation in the sacred act of prayer. I commit to standing firmly, forging a personal relationship with Christ, and discerning your purpose for my life.

9. Lord, in the midst of life's uncertainties and anxieties, I turn to you. Help me find the peace and guidance I need in your presence. Let my prayers be my anchor when decisions weigh heavily on my heart.

10. Heavenly Father, I remember the season in my life when I yearned for change. As I venture into prayer anew, I seek not only answers but a profound sense of peace. Guide me as I recalibrate my life according to your will.

Reflect

19

# The Divine Invitation: Birthing Your Purpose

Sometimes in life, there comes a moment when you realize it's time to push – to birth that dream, that vision, that purpose that has been growing within you. It's like being in labor, feeling the contractions of destiny, and sensing that the time has come to deliver. You might have carried this idea for so long, but now, it's time to take action. And the incredible thing is, you're not doing it alone; you're tapping into the strength of the Almighty.

Understand this truth: anything infused with life, with purpose, comes from God. He is the source of all that is vibrant and meaningful. So, if you feel a deep sense of purpose within you, know that it's a divine spark, a gift from the Creator.

Consider this as your divine invitation to push forward. Maybe you've been pregnant with an idea for years, maybe you've contemplated that ministry, business, or vision for a while now – it's time to deliver it. God is waiting for you to push, and He's not asking for your strength alone but rather for your willingness to act in faith.

Sometimes, all it takes is that one final push, that act of faith, to bring forth what you've been carrying within you. This is your season, your time. When you feel that idea consuming your thoughts day and night, when you can't escape the sense that you're meant for more – that's your cue to push.

Don't be intimidated by the enormity of your vision or the challenges that may lie ahead. Remember, you don't need to have all the resources, plans, or finances in place before you push. This is not about you; it's about aligning yourself with God's purpose. When you push, it's an act of trust, a declaration that you believe God will provide for what He has birthed through you.

I want to be transparent with you; there have been moments in my own life when I've held back due to fear. Fear of the unknown, fear of failure, fear of inadequacy. But I've also learned that when God says it's time, it's time. In those times, I've delved deep into prayer, seeking God's guidance, and when I hear His voice, when I feel that inner prompting, I know it's time to push.

So, I want to encourage you today – push that baby out, push that ministry, business, or vision out into the world. Don't hold back. It's not about being perfect or having it all figured out; it's about obedience and faith. God has entrusted you with something unique, something only you can bring into existence.

You may be amazed at how God takes care of what you birth when you're willing to take that step of faith. Remember, it's His life within you that you're delivering, and He is the one who provides for what He initiates. It's a God thing.

So, take that leap of faith, push that baby out, and watch how God works through your obedience. This is your season, your time to shine, and believe in yourself.

Here's the incredible truth: when you push, it's not just your strength at work; it's God's strength moving through you. You see, anything that God places within you, any purpose or calling that He has birthed in your heart, is beyond human capability. It's beyond what anyone else says or thinks. It's a divine spark that only He can ignite.

So, if you've been carrying a dream, an idea, or a vision for what seems like an eternity, hear this: it's time to deliver. Don't be discouraged by the length of the journey or the challenges you've faced along the way. Remember, God is the one who has planted this purpose within you. He's the author of it all.

It's not about relying on your own strength or trying to have everything perfectly planned out. In fact, you don't need to have all the answers or all the resources in place before you start pushing. This process is not about you; it's about aligning your life with God's purpose. When you push, it's a declaration of your trust in Him.

God is the one who breathes life into your dreams and visions. It doesn't matter what others might say or think; God is the ultimate author of your purpose. You may have been pregnant with ideas, ministries, businesses, or visions for years. Absolutely, pushing that baby out, whether it's birthing your purpose, writing a book, or pursuing your passion, can be incredibly uncomfortable. It often takes everything you've got, and it may not make sense to others who see your gifts and talents. They might assume it's easy, but they don't see the hard work and dedication behind the scenes.

So, to everyone reading this, I join in the chorus: Push that baby out! Embrace the discomfort, stay committed to your purpose, and let your determination carry you through to the incredible fulfillment of your dreams and visions.

Don't be disheartened by the challenges you face along the way. Instead, let them be a testament to your resilience and commitment. Remember, it's the uncomfortable moments that often lead to the most profound growth and achievement.

**Scriptures:**

Proverbs 3:5-6:
*"Trust in the Lord with all your heart, And lean not on your own understanding; In all your ways acknowledge Him, And He shall direct your paths."*

Jeremiah 29:11:
*"For I know the thoughts that I think toward you, says the Lord, thoughts of peace and not of evil, to give you a future and a hope."*

Philippians 4:13:
*"I can do all things through Christ who strengthens me."*

Romans 8:28:
*"And we know that all things work together for good to those who love God, to those who are the called according to His purpose."*

Isaiah 40:31:
*"But those who wait on the Lord Shall renew their strength; They shall mount up with wings like eagles, They shall run and not be weary, They shall walk and*

*not faint."*

Psalm 37:4:

*"Delight yourself also in the Lord, And He shall give you the desires of your heart."*

2 Timothy 1:7:

*"For God has not given us a spirit of fear, but of power and of love and of a sound mind."*

James 1:12:

*"Blessed is the man who endures temptation; for when he has been approved, he will receive the crown of life which the Lord has promised to those who love Him."*

Romans 12:2:

*"And do not be conformed to this world, but be transformed by the renewing of your mind, that you may prove what is that good and acceptable and perfect will of God."*

Psalm 27:14:

*"Wait on the Lord; Be of good courage, And He shall strengthen your heart; Wait, I say, on the Lord!"*

**Prayer Points:**

1. Heavenly Father, I humbly come before You in this moment of realization. I feel the urgency to push forward with the dreams and visions You've placed within me. Grant

me the strength to birth these purposes, knowing that I am not alone, and Your divine spark guides me. Amen.

2. Lord, I acknowledge that all purpose and life come from You. As I contemplate the ministry, business, or vision within me, I accept Your divine invitation to act in faith. Help me push forward in alignment with Your purpose, trusting in Your provision. In Jesus' name, I pray. Amen.

3. Dear God, I recognize that this is my season, my time to deliver what You have placed within me. When I feel consumed by the idea day and night, I trust that it's Your cue to push. Grant me the courage to face the enormity of my vision and the challenges ahead with unwavering faith. Amen.

4. Lord, I confess my past moments of fear and hesitation. Today, I choose to push that ministry, business, or vision into the world. I understand it's not about perfection but obedience and faith. May Your divine guidance lead me as I take this leap of faith. In Your name, I pray. Amen.

5. Heavenly Father, I thank You for entrusting me with something unique. I believe that as I push forward, You will work through my obedience, and I will witness Your divine provision. Strengthen my resolve, Lord, as I embark on this journey. In Jesus' name, I believe and pray. Amen.

6. Lord, I embrace the truth that when I push, it's not my strength but Your divine strength at work. I accept the call to deliver the dreams and purposes You've placed within me, trusting that You are the author of it all. In Your name, I step forward in faith. Amen.

7. Dear God, I've carried these dreams for what feels like an eternity, but I hear Your call to deliver them. I will not be discouraged by the length of the journey or the challenges

I face. I surrender my need for perfect planning and choose to align my life with Your purpose. Strengthen my trust in You, Lord. Amen.

8. Heavenly Father, I recognize that Your breath gives life to my dreams and visions. Regardless of what others may think, I acknowledge that You are the ultimate author of my purpose. Help me push forward, even when it feels uncomfortable, for I know that greatness often emerges from discomfort. In Jesus' name, I pray. Amen.

9. Lord, I join in the chorus with others who are pushing their dreams and purposes forward. I choose to embrace discomfort, stay committed to my purpose, and let determination carry me to the fulfillment of Your plans for me. Strengthen my resolve, Lord. Amen.

10. Dear God, as I face challenges along this journey, may they serve as a testament to my resilience and commitment. Help me remember that it's in uncomfortable moments that I discover my true strength and potential. I trust in Your guidance and provision as I push forward. In Jesus' name, I pray. Amen.

Reflect

# 20

# Pain in Purpose

Pain is an inherent part of the journey towards fulfilling your God-given purpose. As you ignite the fires of your divine vision, it's essential to understand and accept that pain will accompany you on this path. This process can elicit tears, loneliness, sacrifices, and the departure of both possessions and people. The road to purpose can be arduous, lonesome, and trying, but amid these trials, we must hold fast to our focus on the Kingdom of God.

As the Word of God instructs us, *"Seek first the Kingdom of God, and everything else will be added unto you."* This biblical wisdom reminds us to prioritize the Kingdom above all else, especially when facing adversity and pain.

As you read this chapter, meditate on your own life and your perception of what God has called you to do. As you gear up to take the next step in fulfilling your purpose, I encourage you to maintain an unwavering focus on Jesus. This singular devotion will keep you steady, regardless of the trials and tribulations that may come your way.

Embarking on your purpose will require a level of strength,

resources, and abilities that may seem beyond your reach. However, it's crucial to remember that pain is an integral part of this process. Much like my own challenging pregnancy, where I encountered pain, disappointment, and hardship, you too will face moments of despair and uncertainty. But I can testify that through it all, God remained faithful, and His grace sustained me.

In your purpose-driven journey, you'll experience various levels of pain, much like the scale from 0 to 10 that doctors use to gauge discomfort. At times, you may feel little to no pain (0), while other moments may bring a mild (2 or 3) or more substantial (4, 5,...10) degree of anguish. This pain can take different forms—disappointment, emotional hurt, or the loss of relationships. People may let you down, betray your trust, or grow distant from your path. You might need to adjust your surroundings, change your circle of influence, or even undergo personal transformations that cause some to withdraw.

However, I want to reassure you that pursuing your purpose is a journey worth undertaking. Despite the pain, it is through this path that you'll find profound fulfillment. Always remember to keep your gaze fixed on Jesus. Recognize that your purpose is not about you; it's about serving the Kingdom of God and glorifying Him. When you internalize this truth, the trials become more bearable, as you understand that the ultimate goal is for God to receive all the glory—He is God, and He stands alone in His divinity.

Reflect upon the biblical account of Job, a righteous man who faced unimaginable suffering and trials. Job's story is a poignant reminder of how we can navigate pain while seeking our purpose. Job once enjoyed wealth and prosperity but found himself stripped of his riches, health, and loved ones. His questions and struggles during this period were profound, echoing the very queries we may pose when confronted with pain and adversity.

However, the beauty of Job's story lies in his faith and perseverance. Through it all, his unwavering trust in God led to restoration and a deeper understanding of God's divine plan. Just as Job endured and ultimately found meaning and fulfillment, I encourage you to do the same on your journey.

When you encounter pain on your path to purpose, do not shy away from expressing your emotions, seeking support, or even having difficult conversations. Remain steadfast in your faith, unwavering in your commitment to your purpose. Like Job, remember that at the end of the tunnel, there is profound meaning and fulfillment through this transformative journey. Every trial, every tear, and every triumph is an opportunity to give God the praise and honor He deserves.

**Scriptures:**

Matthew 6:33:
*"But seek first the kingdom of God and His righteousness, and all these things shall be added to you."*

Romans 8:18:
*"For I consider that the sufferings of this present time are not worthy to be compared with the glory which shall be revealed in us."*

2 Corinthians 4:17:
*"For our light affliction, which is but for a moment, is*

*working for us a far more exceeding and eternal weight of glory."*

James 1:2-4:
*"My brethren, count it all joy when you fall into various trials, knowing that the testing of your faith produces patience. But let patience have its perfect work, that you may be perfect and complete, lacking nothing."*

Romans 12:12:
*"Rejoicing in hope, patient in tribulation, continuing steadfastly in prayer."*

1 Peter 4:12-13:
*"Beloved, do not think it strange concerning the fiery trial which is to try you, as though some strange thing happened to you; but rejoice to the extent that you partake of Christ's sufferings, that when His glory is revealed, you may also be glad with exceeding joy."*

Psalm 34:17-18:
*"The righteous cry out, and the Lord hears, and delivers them out of all their troubles. The Lord is near to those who have a broken heart, and saves such as have a contrite spirit."*

2 Timothy 2:3:
*"You, therefore, must endure hardship as a good soldier of Jesus Christ."*

1 Corinthians 15:58:

*"Therefore, my beloved brethren, be steadfast, immovable, always abounding in the work of the Lord, knowing that your labor is not in vain in the Lord."*

Isaiah 41:10:

*"Fear not, for I am with you; be not dismayed, for I am your God. I will strengthen you, yes, I will help you, I will uphold you with My righteous right hand."*

**Prayer Points:**

1. Heavenly Father, as I embark on this journey to fulfill my God-given purpose, I recognize that pain is a part of the process. Help me embrace the trials, knowing that You are with me every step of the way.
2. Lord, when tears flow and loneliness surrounds me, remind me that You are my constant companion. May I find solace in Your presence and strength in Your love.
3. Dear God, I understand that sacrifices may be required on this path to purpose. Grant me the courage and wisdom to make these sacrifices willingly, knowing that Your plan is greater than my own desires.
4. Lord Jesus, as people and possessions may depart from my life, help me release them with grace and trust in Your divine plan. Let me not be consumed by loss but rather find comfort in Your eternal promises.
5. Heavenly Father, I pray for the strength to hold fast to my focus on Your Kingdom, even in the face of adversity and pain. Let Your Kingdom be my anchor and my purpose's

guiding light.

6. Gracious God, I meditate on Your Word, *"Seek first the Kingdom of God."* Help me prioritize Your Kingdom above all else, especially when life's challenges seem overwhelming.

7. Lord, I fix my unwavering gaze upon Jesus as I pursue my purpose. May His example of steadfast devotion inspire me to persevere through every trial and tribulation.

8. Heavenly Father, I acknowledge that this journey may require resources and abilities beyond my current reach. Grant me the faith to trust that You will provide what is needed in Your perfect timing.

9. Lord, I pray for resilience in the face of disappointment and emotional hurt. Help me understand that these moments of pain are opportunities for growth and reliance on Your grace.

10. God of restoration, as I navigate the various levels of pain on this purpose-driven journey, let me remember the story of Job. May his faith and perseverance serve as a testament to the fulfillment that awaits those who trust in You. Amen.

Reflect

# 21

# Legacy of Faith: Passing the Torch of Belief

Fulfilling one's purpose is a profound self-reward. The sensation of walking in alignment with your purpose is exhilarating. It feels like you are not only accomplishing what God has called you to do but also contributing to something greater than yourself—a legacy. The story of Abraham in the Bible exemplifies the significance of fulfilling one's purpose and the transformative influence of obedience in one's journey, especially in shaping future generations.

In the Scriptures, Abraham received a divine call, accompanied by God's promise to bless him and make his name renowned. Throughout the book of Genesis, Abraham's unwavering obedience led him on a faith-filled journey. As he pursued his purpose, God established a covenant with him, reaffirming the promise of inheritance.

Remarkably, Abraham and his wife Sarah, despite their advanced age and her barrenness, miraculously welcomed a son. This event ultimately led to Isaac becoming the father of Jacob, from whom the 12 tribes of Israel descended. Abraham's obedience birthed a generational legacy that we should not underestimate. As we navigate our own earthly purposes, let us recognize the spiritual inheritance we accumulate along the way. Abraham's narrative should serve as a source of inspiration, encouraging us to have faith throughout our purpose-driven journey and to diligently follow God's call, thereby fulfilling our unique purpose in this life.

As you journey toward fulfilling your purpose, remember that your purpose extends beyond yourself—it allows you to pass down faith to those around you and the next generation. When others see that God has worked through you, it inspires them to believe that He can work in their lives too. Thus, fulfilling your purpose becomes a means of imparting faith, creating a foundation of spiritual strength for the future.

Whether you have children, siblings, students, or others looking up to you, understand that your actions and faith don't just impact you but also shape the lives of those who follow. In Deuteronomy 6:6-7, we are reminded of the importance of impressing God's commandments on our hearts and sharing them with our children, teaching them in our daily lives.

Furthermore, fulfilling your purpose opens doors for mentoring and discipleship, aligning with the example set by Jesus and His disciples. Jesus not only taught through words but also through His actions, lifestyle, and character, investing time and energy in the personal growth of His followers. As you experience blessings on your journey, recognize that you have the capacity to bless others too. In your pursuit of purpose, remember to give back to your community and the people God has placed in your life. Share the knowledge and blessings you've received, just as you were once taught and blessed.

As we navigate our individual paths of purpose, it's crucial to ensure that God's transformative work continues to impact lives and advance His kingdom. Following the example of Jesus, we must not only pursue our own purpose but also create space to invest in the growth and development of others. This involves mentoring and discipling others in biblical principles, leaving behind a legacy of faith and transformation.

It's important to recognize that shaping a legacy is an ongoing process that demands dedication, consistency, and a deep commitment to living out our faith and values in Christ. As we strive to fulfill our purposes, love ourselves, seek God's guidance, serve others, and educate ourselves, we must also remain open to continuous adjustment so that the kingdom of God can manifest as it needs to. Our journey of purpose should be marked by intentional actions that perpetuate positive change and growth.

**Scriptures:**

Proverbs 19:21:
*"There are many plans in a man's heart, nevertheless the Lord's counsel—that will stand."*

Ephesians 2:10:
*"For we are His workmanship, created in Christ Jesus for good works, which God prepared beforehand that we should walk in them."*

2 Timothy 1:9:
*"Who has saved us and called us with a holy calling, not according to our works, but according to His own purpose*

and grace which was given to us in Christ Jesus before time began."

Romans 8:28:

"And we know that all things work together for good to those who love God, to those who are the called according to His purpose."

Proverbs 20:5:

"Counsel in the heart of man is like deep water, but a man of understanding will draw it out."

Psalm 57:2:

"I will cry out to God Most High, to God who performs all things for me."

Proverbs 3:5-6:

"Trust in the Lord with all your heart, and lean not on your own understanding; in all your ways acknowledge Him, and He shall direct your paths."

2 Corinthians 9:8:

"And God is able to make all grace abound toward you, that you, always having all sufficiency in all things, may have an abundance for every good work."

Matthew 28:19-20:

"Go therefore and make disciples of all the nations, baptizing them in the name of the Father and of the Son and of the Holy Spirit, teaching them to observe all things *that I have commanded you; and lo, I am with you always, even to the end of the age."*

Romans 15:13:

*"Now may the God of hope fill you with all joy and peace in believing, that you may abound in hope by the power of the Holy Spirit."*

**Prayer Points:**

1. Heavenly Father, I come before You with gratitude for the purpose You've placed in my heart. Help me understand that fulfilling this purpose is a self-reward that aligns me with Your divine plan.
2. Lord, as I walk in alignment with my purpose, I feel the exhilaration of knowing I'm contributing to something greater than myself—a legacy that glorifies Your name. Guide me along this path.
3. Dear God, I'm inspired by the story of Abraham, his unwavering obedience, and the generational legacy it birthed. Strengthen my faith as I pursue my own purpose-driven journey.
4. Lord, I recognize that my purpose extends beyond myself. Grant me the wisdom and compassion to pass down faith to those around me and the next generation.
5. Heavenly Father, as I fulfill my purpose, may my actions inspire others to believe in Your transformative power. Let my life be a testimony of Your grace.
6. God, I pray for the children, siblings, students, and all

those who look up to me. Help me impress Your command-ments on their hearts and be a source of spiritual strength for their future.

7. Lord Jesus, I'm thankful for Your example of mentoring and discipleship. Teach me to invest in the growth and development of others as I experience Your blessings on my journey.

8. Heavenly Father, may I be a source of blessings to those You've placed in my life. Help me give back, share knowl-edge, and nurture the potential of others just as I have been taught and blessed.

9. Lord, shape me into a vessel that perpetuates positive change and growth. May my actions align with Your kingdom's advancement, leaving behind a legacy of faith and transformation.

10. God, grant me the dedication and consistency needed to shape a lasting legacy. Help me remain open to Your guidance and adjustments, ensuring that Your kingdom manifests as You intend through my purpose-driven jour-ney.

## Reflect

www.ingramcontent.com/pod-product-compliance
Lightning Source LLC
Chambersburg PA
CBHW060929140726
47996CB00001B/437